The Lottery Solution

by William Atwood

RIVERCROSS PUBLISHING, INC,
NEW YORK, NEW YORK

1992

ISBN: 0-944957-13-7

First Printing

Library of Congress Cataloging-in-Publication Data

Atwood, William L.
    The lottery solution/by William Atwood.
      p. cm.
    ISBN 0-944957-13-7: $9.95
    1. Lotteries. I. Title
HG6111.A85 1992
795—dc20

                                   92-560
                                     CIP

Table of Contents

Preface ... 1

Foreword ... 3

Introduction   Facts, Myths, Questions ... 5

Chapter 1   The Language of Lotteries ... 9

Chapter 2   Welcome to "Lotto 101" ... 13

Chapter 3   Random Selection: Why it Doesn't Work ... 21

Chapter 4   Numeric Systems and Their Limitations ... 28

Chapter 5   Methods That Improve Odds ... 35

Chapter 6   How to Select Numbers ... 44

Chapter 7   Can Lotteries Be Fixed? ... 51

Supplement One ... 59

Appendix 1   40 Line Samples ... 61

Appendix 2   Lottery Fever/Social Programs ... 83

Bibliography ... 85

Table 1   Random Distribution of Lottery Formats ... 86

Table 2   Probability that Numbers Will Occur, Not Occur, Repeat on Next Line ... 92

Table 3   Average Numbers Represented: Random vs. Matrix ... 93

Table 3A: Average Numbers Represented by Random Selection ... 94

Table 3B: Average Repeat Numbers by Random Selection ... 96

Table 3C: Missing Numbers by Random Selection ... 97

Table 4   Odds of All Winning Numbers OccuringWithin Multiple-Line Bets ... ·98

Table 5   The Real Cost of a Chance to Win! ... 102

Preface

My discovery of these methods is a direct result of a speeding ticket: One Tuesday in February, while driving home from work during a snowstorm, my car became stuck in the snow. While I was waiting for a tow truck, the Police came by and gave me a "speeding ticket." (This did not put me in the best of moods!) On Wednesday, our state lottery jackpot was worth twenty million dollars. The State Lottery Commissioner attended the drawing to give an annual report on the earnings of the State Lottery. The State had made over half a billion dollars, but there were many fewer winners than I expected. On Thursday a member of our lottery club at work dropped 40 losing lottery tickets on my desk and challenged me to "find a better way."

I would not have looked at those tickets but I was still angry about that speeding ticket, and disturbed at the lottery report. All 40 lottery tickets were "easy picks." I discovered that one of the six winning numbers didn't occur anywhere within the 40 tickets. I began to wonder if this is likely to occur per random selection or, can it be manipulated by a lottery operator? And if the number distributions can be controlled to benefit lottery operators(fewer winners)? Can they also be changed to improve the odds for lottery players(more winners)?

Several months later, that speeding ticket was dismissed. However, the court had given me further incentive to write this book. They had called me "stupid," and made comments about my "alleged I.Q. of 190." I later found out why I had received that "speeding ticket." I had worked for the uncle of one of the cops. The uncle's paint company went out of business. The uncle lost all of his millions, and committed suicide. the cop didn't inherit any of those millions, and blames former employees for the failure of her uncle's paint company. this coincidence provided more incentive to write this book.

I do have some goals and objectives for *The Lottery Solution:*

A. Create more lottery winners and millionaires than anyone else in history.

B. Build a "billion-dollar" wall with photocopies of winning tickets using these methods. (I'm asking winners to send photocopies.)

C. I am hopeful that thousands will buy scientific calculators to examine the concepts introduced herein, and in the process will expand their knowledge, and the applications of mathematics in their lives manyfold.

D. I'd like to meet those who use my methods and win. I like to take a Caribbean cruise every few months. Write, and I'll tell you my favorite ships (and routes). Maybe we can charter an entire cruise ship for my winners?

Foreword

This is a technical reference book dealing with improving odds of winning lotteries. It is not to be confused with "supermarket tabloids" which promise "winning numbers" or "lottery-systems" which do little more than move numbers around from line to line. Such systems can win, but their odds of winning are no better than random.

The object of the game is to have enough winning numbers on the same line to win. That is what lottery is all about. Yet most of you buy your tickets with little thought of the objective. The average lottery wager is for five dollars. Yet in California, Illinois, and New York, about 226 out of 227 players who buy five tickets have *no chance* to win! That's right; 226 out of 227 players don't have a chance to hit a HOME RUN because they didn't make the team and won't get a chance to go to bat! Methods in this book will get more of you into the game, and therefore more HOME RUNS (lottery winners). In some formats we can give every lottery player a chance to get into the game rather than just a chance to watch.

I not only give you the facts; but when you finish this book, you will be able to do almost any lottery calculation for yourself. I do all the math, but show how it is done, and teach you how to use it for your own applications.

3

If you want to follow my calculations, you will need a calculator with "combinations" key (nCr) and "random" (RND). You can find them for ten dollars and up. (Read the book first to decide if you require one.)

I recommend reading this book at least twice. The information in earlier chapters will have more meaning if you have read later chapters. Information all ties together, and I can't present all of it to you at the same time.

I used to buy just one "easy-pick" lottery ticket whenever the jackpot got to about 8 million. One day (See Preface) I found a reason to sit down and do some research on lotteries. Now that I've found methods to increase the odds of winning, I have a decision: Do I distribute these methods and have more lottery winners, or do I allow the lottery operators to make more money? (Appendix 2)

In the spirit of Robin Hood, I want to see more lottery winners. Lottery operators won't lose money if we create more winners—they just won't make as much. I want to create more lottery winners (and more millionaires) than anyone else in history, and doing it by giving away the states' money only makes my smile bigger. After all—I'm not giving away my money!

Good Luck and Best Wishes.
William Atwood

Introduction

There are 43,252,003,274,489,856,000 possible configurations of Rubik's cube. The most complicated non-Multiple Draw lottery (90/5 format) has only 43,949,268 possible combinations. The cube is 984,134,781,700 times more complex than the most complicated lottery. (Note: The most complicated non-Multiple Draw lottery format used in the United States is 54/6 format, with 25,827,165 possible combinations. By comparison, the cube is 1,674,670,963,000 times more complex.) Within months of its introduction, several books began appearing with solutions to the cube. Lotteries have been around for years, yet there have been no real solutions offered! Until now, *there was nothing that really improved the odds of winning!*

Why have there been no real solutions offered for lotteries? You can hold a cube in your hand; look at it; manipulate it; even begin to understand it. You can have a real cube in front of you; you don't need a mathematical model. Until now, No one has created mathematical models of lotteries and solved them to improve odds of winning. If you create mathematical models of lotteries, take them apart and put them back together to see how they work, then you can examine methods that can really improve the odds of winning.

Before getting into the text; I'd like to address a few myths about lotteries, and questions about this publication.

Sales for 29 U.S. lottery states are over $20,000,000,000 per year, and are growing. (Almost $400 million per week.) The average bet is for five dollars. Most lotteries have drawings twice a week. This works out to 40 million people betting five dollars on a lottery twice each week. Lotteries in France, Spain, and Germany total over 7 billion dollars per year; this doesn't include the rest of Europe.

Question: I don't want to read your book, or examine your methods. Just tell me the winning numbers.

Answer: You missed the point. Every so-called "lottery book" tells you "winning-numbers." They don't work!

Question: I just want to know how to improve my odds of winning? You don't have to explain them or tell how you discovered them. Just tell me how I can improve my odds.

Answer: Methods are in Chapter 5. How to select numbers in Chapter 6.

Myth: Odds of winning a lottery are what they are, and there is no way of changing them.

Fact: I used to believe that too! And, it is true if you buy only one ticket. The fact is: few lottery players buy only one ticket. With more than one ticket—there are lots of things we can do to improve the odds.

Myth: Most lottery players are casual players.

Fact: 70% of all lottery players bet on almost every lottery. "Casual" players come in as jackpots get bigger.

Myth: Most players have their own "systems" which they use religiously.

Fact: 90% of all numbers are chosen by state lottery computers. ("easy-picks")

Myth: 90% of all lottery winners won with "easy-picks,"

therefore they are best way to win.

Fact: 90% of tickets sold are "easy-picks." If they were a good method, they would account for more than 90% of winners.

Question: You say the way to improve odds of winning is to make mathematical models and solve them. Do you present models of actual lotteries?

Answer: I have created 3 lottery formats, and present models in their entirety. I wish I could use actual state lottery formats; however, the smallest format (35/5) would require 2,706 pages. The 54/6 format would take 215,227 pages. That 90/5 format used in Europe requires 366,244 pages. Please note: I do summarize actual distributions of all lottery formats—this is the important point.

Question: Your random odds are based on tickets priced at $1 each. Aren't odds halved when tickets are sold at 2 for a dollar, etc? The 54/6 format is 25,827,165 to 1 odds; but is 12,913,583 to 1 odds when you buy 2 tickets.

Answer: No! When you buy 2 tickets, the odds are 25,827,165 to 1 for each ticket. Odds do not change, unless you use methods that affect the odds of winning—such as described in this book. Note: It is actually possible to lessen odds by buying more tickets!

Question: I'm not good at math, and why do you have so many tables?

Answer: I don't try to teach you math. I do introduce some concepts you probably have not considered before; and allow you to look at lotteries in ways you've never looked at before. I do all calculations for you, but show you how they are done.

Question: What are your motives in publishing these methods?

Answer: I want to re-distribute the lottery wealth. There are not enough winners, and those who win, win too much! I want to see more people share the money.

I know how to increase the number of lottery winners several times. These methods will soon account for a majority of winners in every format and state. I want to keep a scoresheet to that effect. If you use these methods and win, I want to know about it. Also tell me which method in Chapter 6 you used to select numbers. Just a note or postcard with format and state will do. If possible, send a photocopy of your winning ticket. I have this wall I'd like to decorate with a BILLION DOLLARS worth of winning tickets. (I'm serious about this! With publication of this book, it won't take long.) You don't have to sign your name or give a return address. If you have any questions, send a SSAE to the address below, or to the publisher, and I'll try to answer.

William L. Atwood
P.O. Box 2639
Detroit MI. 48151

Chapter

1

The Language of Lotteries

Glossary

Bingo Lottery	use of bingo numbers to select lottery numbers.
"easy-pick"	number-combinations chosen by lottery computer.
Format	total numbers/numbers drawn. i.e. 40/6 is: 40 pick 6. (6 numbers selected from 40.)
Lottery (Lotto)	contest in which winners are drawn by lot.
Lottery Chips	use of numbered chips (i.e. poker chips) to select number-combinations.
Lottery Cube	use of numbered cube to select number-combinations.
Lottery Darts	dartboard painted with lottery numbers and used to select number-combinations.
Lottery Sticks	use of numbered sticks to select number-combinations.
Matrix Methods	method of selecting number-combinations

which limits the number of times losing numbers can occur, and optimizes the ratio of winning numbers to losing numbers.

Multiple-draw Lottery Lottery in which winning numbers are drawn from more than one source.

Numeric Systems statistical sampling "technique" used to select number-combinations.

nCr mathematical expression for combinations, which doesn't consider order of selection. n=numbers in field. r=numbers drawn. i.e.: 36C6=1,947,792 combinations.

nPr mathematical expression for combinations, in which the order of selection is considered. i.e.: 36P6=1,402,410,240 combinations. (Note: For lotteries, the following ratios will always apply: 120 times nC5=nP5 720 times nC6=nP6 5,040 times nC7=nP7.)

"Power-Ball" see Multiple Draw.

Random Selection any way of selecting number-combinations which has no overall effect on odds of winning.

Random Repetition propensity of a losing number to also occur on following line, thus defeating both lines. (also called: "Random-Creep" and "Creep-Factor")

roll-over when no one wins; jackpot rolls-over into next drawing, thereby greatly increasing that jackpot.

Single-number (also called "one-number") method of selecting numbers in which a number occurs only one time in a set number of lines. (See Matrix Methods)

Short-term Random Distribution	disproportionate distribution of numbers in random selections, which assures a poor distribution of winning numbers.
"/"	3 uses: A) Used to designate lottery format, such as 36/6 or 54/6 formats. B) Jackpot winners such as 6/6 or 7/7 winner. Other winners such as 4/6 or 5/6 winners. C) Used in calculations as symbol for division. i.e.: 42/6=7.

Combinations

You must have some understanding of combinations before you can begin to understand lotteries. Suppose I give you the numbers 1 through 3, and ask how many combinations of 2 numbers you can make? Let's list all the combinations: 1,2; 2,3; and 1,3. There are no other combinations of 2 numbers to be made from these numbers. There are 3 combinations of 2 numbers that can be made from 3 numbers. It can also be expressed in the following ways: 3C2=3 possible combinations; and (3/2) times (2/1)=3 combinations.

Now, how many combinations of 2 numbers can be made from numbers 1 through 5? Let's do it: 1,2; 1,3; 1,4; 1,5; 2,3; 2,4; 2,5; 3,4; 3,5; and 4,5. There are no other combinations of 2 numbers that can be made from these 5 numbers. It is also true that from any 5 numbers only 10 combinations of 2 numbers can be made. Thus, 5C2=10 combinations; or (5/2) times (4/1)=10 combinations.

Suppose we make those combinations of 3-numbers rather than 2-numbers? We have: 1,2,3; 1,2,4; 1,2,5; 1,3,4; 1,3,5; 1,4,5; 2,3,4; 2,3,5; 2,4,5; and 3,4,5. From 5 numbers, there are 10 combinations of 3 numbers. Thus, 5C3=10; and (5/3) times (4/2) times (3/1)=10. Notice that both 5C2 and 5C3 equal 10 combinations! Combinations don't work like other mathematical functions. Consider all the possible combinations we can make from **Five Numbers:**

5CN	Combinations	Comments
5C0=1	/12345/	1 set of 5 numbers.
5C1=5	1/2/3/4/5	5 combinations of 1 number.
5C2=10	12/13/14/15/23 24/25/34/35/45	10 combinations of 2 numbers.
5C3=10	123/124/125/134/135 145/234/235/245/345	10 combinations of 3 numbers.
5C4=5	1234/1235/1345 2345/1245	5 combinations of 4 numbers.
5C5=1	12345	1 combination of 5 numbers.

Notice the distribution, with the maximum number of combinations in the middle. You're probably asking yourself: "That's all very nice—but what does it have to do with improving my odds of winning lotteries?" We are defining the "bits and pieces" that make up lotteries. Let's examine how combinations occur with some other numbers:

Six Numbers

6Cn	Combinations	Comments
6C0=1	1	1 set of 6 numbers.
6C1=6	6	6 combinations of 1-number.
6C2=15	15	15 combinations of 2-numbers.
6C3=20	20	20 combinations of 3-numbers.
6C4=15	15	15 combinations of 4-numbers.
6C5=6	6	6 combinations of 5-numbers.
6C6=1	1	1 combination of 6-numbers.

Results are different from combinations of five numbers, but the distribution is similar. Note that largest number of combinations is at the mid-point. This is a function of all combinations. Examples follow:

Eight Numbers	Ten Numbers
8C0=1	10C0=1
8C1=8	10C1=10
8C2=28	10C2-45
8C3=56	10C3=120
8C4=70	10C4=210
8C5=56	10C5=252
8C6=28	10C6=210
8C7=8	10C7=120
8C8=1	10C8=45
	10C9=10
	10C10=1

The largest number of combinations will be at the mid-point, dropping to 1 at each end. This "standard-distribution" is a function of all combinations. All lottery formats are made up of combinations similar to these, and these lottery formats have definite distributions from which mathematical models can be made. Look at a 54 number lottery:

Combinations

54C0, and 54C54	1
54C1, and 54C53	54
54C2, and 54C52	1,431
54C3, and 54C51	24,806
54C4, and 54C50	316,251
54C5, and 54C49	3,162,510
54C6, and 54C48	25,827,165
and up to	
54C27 (mid-point)	1,946,939,426,000,000

We have deleted many numbers from the above example, but the pattern is clear. Note the odds of a 54/6 lottery are 25,827,165 to 1. There are 25,827,165 possible combinations of 6-numbers that can be made from 54 numbers. If we set up a lottery to select 48 numbers from 54, the odds of winning are also 25,827,165 to 1! How can this be? In 54/6, we are selecting 6 numbers. In 54/48, we are leaving 6 numbers. These formats are mirror-images of each other. One is the print; the other is the negative.

By now, I hope you're wondering: "If there are millions of possible combinations, and thus odds of millions to 1, how do we go about improving our odds of winning?" Can we do something different? Something that has not yet been done on a large scale?

The United States Chamber of Commerce, in conjunction with its Malcom Baldridge Quality Award, recommends 4 ways for American companies to improve quality and efficiency. In the following chapters, we apply these to lotteries. These recommended ways to improve are: (In increasing level of efficiency)

1. **Try Harder**
2. **Emulate (copy)**
3. **Leapfrog**
4. **Change the Rules of the Game**

We have looked at the concept of "combinations," which is the groundwork upon which lotteries are based. We will look into the structures of lottery formats to see what "makes them work," examine Random Selection to see why it doesn't work, and look into the logic of "lottery-systems" (numeric-systems), which have been around for centuries, to see limitations of these methods. Finally, we will "change the rules of the game," and look into methods that do affect the odds of winning!

Welcome to "Lotto 101"

To understand how lotteries work, let's set up our own lottery. How does a 6/3 format sound? It has only 20 possible combinations (6C3=20), and would be perfect to use at the office or around the neighborhood. Here is a model of our 6/3 lottery:

Numbers: 1-2-3-4-5-6

Possible Combinations:

1) 123	2) 124	3) 125	4) 126
5) 134	6) 135	7) 136	8) 145
9) 146	10) 156	11) 234	12) 235
13) 236	14) 245	15) 246	16) 256
17) 345	18) 346	19) 356	20) 456

Around the office we can probably sell 8 to 10 tickets per each drawing; this will give about a 40% chance that someone will win. (20 number-combinations divided by 10 tickets sold minus a couple of duplicated tickets equals approximately 8 number-combinations played.) No matter what the winning number-combination is, there is only 1 of the 20 number-combinations that will contain all 3 winning numbers. We will have a problem with giving a prize for 2 winning numbers: 9

of the 20 number-combinations will have 2 of the winning numbers. There are also 9 number-combinations that have 1 of the winning numbers, but only 1 number-combination that has none of the winning numbers:

Winning-Numbers	Combinations	Percent
3	1	5%
2	9	45%
1	9	45%
0	1	5%

We have set up our lottery and sold tickets; now we have our first drawing. First ball rolls out, it's number 3, followed by number 1, and number 2. Our winning number is; 1-2-3, since we don't consider order of selection. (Note, if order of selection is considered, 312 is the winning number, and there are 120 possible combinations, since 6P3=120. Here, order of selection is not considered, so 6C3=20.) Let's take a look at results of our drawing:

Number-Combinations

Results

1 2 3

(1) number-combination with all 3 winning-numbers.

1 2 4, 1 2 5, 1 2 6
1 3 4, 1 3 5, 1 3 6
2 3 4, 2 3 5, 2 3 6

(9) number-combinations with 2 winning numbers.

1 4 5, 1 4 6, 1 5 6
2 4 5, 2 4 6, 2 5 6
3 4 5, 3 4 6, 3 5 6

(9) number-combinations with 1 winning-number.

4 5 6

(1) number-combination with no winning-numbers.

This 6/3 format will always have the above distribution, no matter what the winning numbers are! In fact, every lottery format has its own unique distribution which never changes! The jackpot winner in our drawing will have all 3 winning numbers—and will receive 50% of the money collected. Second prize (20%) will go to whoever didn't have any of the winning numbers. (90% willl have either one or two of the winning numbers, but only 5% will have none of the numbers.)

After a few weeks, interest in our little 6/3 lottery increased, and the whole 2nd floor was playing it. This increased sales to about 20 tickets per drawing, and decreased our probability of a roll-over to about 35%. There was now a 65% probability our lottery would be won. Then, the first floor started buying tickets. We were then selling about 40 tickets per drawing. This made the odds of someone winning our lottery at about 85%. Odds of it rolling-over and increasing the jackpot were now about nil.

With odds of someone winning our lottery so high (85%), we began looking for another format. We added a couple of numbers to make an 8/3 format lottery. Odds on this new 8/3 lottery are 56 to 1. (8C3=56) The 56 possible number-combinations in this format range from: 1. 1-2-3...thru...56. 6-7-8. This 8/3 format will always have the following distribution:

Winning-Numbers	Combinations	Percent
3	One	1.7%
2	15	26.8%
1	30	53.5%
0	10	17.8%

Within the first couple of drawings, we found a few shortcomings with this format. Those with two winning numbers felt they weren't receiving as much as they deserved. Most winners with 2 numbers usually got their money back—but little more. We usually sold about 40 tickets on a first drawing, with 50% going to the jackpot, 20% to the pool for second place, and 30% going to lottery operators. That breaks down to $20 to jackpot, $8 to second place pool, and $12 to lottery operator. When we sold 40 tickets, we had 8 to 10 second place winners sharing an $8 pool. Somehow they didn't consider themselves as winners. This didn't improve when we had a roll-over. We averaged around 60 tickets after a roll-over, with a jackpot worth $50 ($20 plus 1/2 of 60,) and a second place pool now worth about $12—but split between 14 to 16 second—place winners! Notice that the pool for second place is only 20% of total money, but the 15 possible number-combinations with 2 winning numbers comprise 26.8% of all number-combinations! At this rate, we will usually have more winners than money. So, we had to change to another format.

Now we tried a 10/3 format with 120 possible number-combination: 1. 1-2-3...thru...120. 8-9-10. This 10/3 format will always have following distribution:

Winning-Numbers	Combinations	Percent
3	One	0.8%
2	21	17.5%
1	63	52.5%
0	35	29.2%

We are treating our second place winners a little better with this format: 20% of the money is being distributed to 17.5% who have 2 winning numbers. (21 of the 120 number-combinations.)

Now let's look at a real format used by states.*

Take a 36/6 format for example: It will have 1,947,792 possible number-combinations. (36C6=1,947,792) Distribution will always be as follows:

Winning-Numbers	Combinations	Percent	Odds to 1
6	One	0.0000051	1,947,792
5	180	0.0092	10,821
4	6,625	0.335	299
3	81,200	4.169	24
2	411,075	21.105	4.7
1	855,036	43.898	2.3
0	593,775	30.485	3.3
TOTALS	**1,947,792**	**100.00**	

If tickets are sold on a random basis, the results will be very close to this distribution. If we sell one million tickets chosen by random, we expect 92 5-number winners (1,000,000 times .000092), 3,350 4-number winners (1,000,000 times .00335).

*Distributions of all lottery formats are included in tables.

However, don't expect a 51% probability that the jackpot will be won. (1,000,000/1,947,792) Because of duplicate number-combinations being sold, this logic doesn't apply to the jackpot number! The probability of the jackpot being won is: total number combinations sold (not tickets sold) divided by total number-combinations. Due to duplicate number-combinations being sold, the probability of the jackpot being won in our 36/6 format lottery is only about 40% when 1,000,000 tickets are sold. When the number of tickets sold equals the total number-combinations of the lottery format (i.e. 1,947,792 tickets in 36/6 lottery); there is only about a 62.5% probability of the jackpot being won. Probability of the jackpot being won can be expressed by the following ratios:

Number of tickets sold as percent of total number-combinations	Percentage of number-combinations selected
25%	22% *22.1*
50%	40% *39,4*
100%	62.5% *63.2*
200%	85% *86.5*

Duplication of number-combinations makes the jackpot number more elusive than other number-combinations because there is only one jackpot number. For example, of the 92 5-number winners, we do not expect that 92 different number-combinations will be represented. We would expect that about 72 5/6 number-combinations will occur (40% of 180), but because of duplicate, about 20 will repeat to give total of 92. There are 92 5/6 winners, but only 72 of possible 180 5/6 number-combinations (40%) have been chosen. Expect the same with 4/6 winners, and other levels of distribution. the complete picture looks as follows:

36/6 Format—1,000,000 Tickets Sold

36/6	Possible Combinations	Possible Combinations Sold	# Tickets Sold
6/6	1	0	0
5/6	180	72	92
4/6	6,525	2,610	3,350
3/6	81,200	32,480	41,688
2/6	411,075	164,430	211,047
1/6	855,036	342,014	438,978
0/6	593,775	237,510	304,845
TOTAL	1,947,792	779,116	1,000,000
Percent	100%	40%	51%

At this level (tickets sold=51% of total possible number-combinations) approximately 22% of all tickets sold are duplicates. This increases as more tickets are sold. The next ticket sold (#1,000,001) has a 40% probability of being a duplicate of one of the 779,116 combinations already sold. (779,116/1,947,792)

For comparison let's see how our 36/6 lottery looks when we sell 3,896,000 tickets (200% of the total 1,947,792 possible number-combinations):

36/6 Format—3,896,000 Tickets Sold

36/6	Possible Combinations	Possible Combinations Sold	# Tickets Sold
6/6	1	1	2
5/6	180	153	360
4/6	6,525	5,546	13,051
3/6	81,200	69,020	162,417
2/6	411,075	349,414	822,238
1/6	855,036	726,781	1,710,255
0/6	593,775	504,709	1,187,677
TOTAL	1,947,792	1,655,624	3,896,000
Percent	100%	85%	200%

Notice the differences between these two levels of play. The number of possible combinations doesn't change; this is a function of the lottery format, and will always remain constant. that is, there will always be 411,075 possible combinations with 2 winning numbers in 36/6 format. There is a relationship between the number of tickets sold and number-combinations sold. When the number of tickets sold is 50% of possible-combinations, then approximately 40% of the possible number-combinations have been sold. When the number of tickets sold is 200% of possible combinations, then approximately 85% of all number-combinations have been sold.

At 1 million tickets sold there is only a 40% chance that the jackpot number-combination has been sold even though the tickets sold carry 51% of combinations. This is because only 40% of the possible number-combinations have been sold. At 3,896,000 tickets sold; there is an 85% probability that the jackpot number combination has been sold, and at this level it is most likely that it has been sold twice! (2 winners) If number selections are random, there will be little variance in these distributions. The 10% of all lottery players who choose their own numbers can have little effect on the distribution in any lottery format.

Conclusion—Chapter 2

Even though number-combinations and jackpot numbers are selected by random selection, there is a definite distribution within a lottery. This distribution does not change! No matter which format is used, there is always one jackpot number, a certain number of 5/6 winners, a certain number of 4/6 winners, etc. Even a roulette wheel is a definite lottery format. (38/1 in the USA; 37/1 elsewhere.) The percentage of number-combinations sold can be calculated from the number of tickets sold as it is a ratio, and applies to every lottery format! If we know the number of tickets sold, we can compute the expected distribution; and this will be very close, as only 10%

choose their numbers; the other 90% are random selection. Results of lotteries have predictable distribution. How else could operators run them? But it is possible to improve on these predictable results!

Chapter

3

Random Selection: Why it Doesn't Work.

The next three chapters are based on methods of play that: A) Have no effect on odds of winning; B) May affect odds of winning under certain circumstances; and C) Methods that do improve odds of winning. This chapter examines "methods" most of you use to select number-combinations, and explains why they don't work.

It's very frustrating to watch most of you buy lottery tickets. If you bought a jigsaw puzzle and half the pieces were missing, you'd probably want your money back. If you went fishing, you'd probably want to put some kind of bait on your hook. Yet, most of you buy lottery tickets as if you're buying that jigsaw puzzle with missing pieces—and seem perfectly happy about it! If you knew a better way, you'd probably use it. Here are the "methods" most of you use. These account for about 99% of all lottery tickets sold.

"Any Number"

Any number is as good as any other number—so what difference does it make what my numbers are? These players have committed themselves to believing there is nothing better than random selection, or, if there is, they don't know what it is. Most common of the "any-number" systems are the number-combinations chosen by state lottery computers. These numbers are called several things: "lucky-numbers," "quick-picks," "auto-lotto," and "easy-picks" among other terms. I don't know of any reasons why they might be "lucky," but they are quick, auto, and easy, so I call all lottery computer generated numbers "easy-picks." These computer chosen "easy-picks" account for about 90% of all tickets sold!

"Aunt Lucy's Birthday"

These players use birthdays and other significant dates to determine their numbers. Although these "significant" numbers are not chosen by random means, chances of them winning are no better than random. In fact, since there are no birthdays later than the 31st, any number over 31 defeats this means of selecting numbers. Ages within a family or group of friends may not be as representative as birthdays. This is the second most popular "system" for selecting numbers.

"Historical System"

This system has two variations. Each variation considers which numbers have won in previous lottery drawings. One variation considers that the trend of winning numbers will continue, and thus selects those numbers which have won most in the past. The other variation considers that in the long run all numbers will be drawn an equal number of times, and selects those numbers which won the fewest number of times in past lotteries. Chances of winning with these "systems" is no better than random. One of these principles may hold true in the short run, the other in the long run; but chances of continuing a trend or averaging it out on any given lottery drawing are no better than random.

"The Great Zippy Zolton"

These systems select numbers on the basis of Astrological, or Numerological significance. These are usually books of "lucky" or "hot" numbers. These books usually have "disclaimers" that do not guarantee any results better than random selection. If these systems worked, more people would be winning lotteries. Plus, if they did work, how many players would have to share the jackpot because they all played the same "hot" number?

"One Ticket"

Although the average lottery wager is for five dollars, there are some who buy only one ticket. This "one-ticket" system can make use of any system mentioned above. Odds of winning can never be better than random—one chance in the total number-combinations of lottery format!

"Why Random Selection Doesn't Work"

Random selection doesn't work because it doesn't allow a distribution of numbers that offers a chance to win! Since the average bet is for five dollars, let's select five number combinations by random selection:

36/6 Format

Line #1	2-5-**12**-**17**-26-34
#2	3-**12**-15-**17**-18-**23**
#3	8-**12**-14-**23**-27-29
#4	7-11-15-28-35-36
#5	10-13-14-19-33-34

(Note: numbers in **bold** are numbers that repeat on the next line. This notation will be continued throughout this book and its significance will be discussed later in this chapter.)

What is the probability that one of our tickets will win? It is 36C6=1,947,792 to 1 (Chapter 1, remember?) What is the probability that we even have all 6 of the winning numbers within our 5 tickets above? **If we don't have all the winning numbers; we can't win!**

We have 23 of the possible 36 numbers in our five tickets above. Thirteen of the 36 numbers don't occur. If one of these 13 missing numbers (1,4,6,9,16,20,21,22,24,25,30,31,32) is among the winning numbers, **we lose!** The odds of having all

6 winning numbers is (35C6)/(23C6)=5%, or 20 to 1 odds that we don't have all 6 winning numbers. That is really quite good for this format. On average, only 20 of the 36 numbers will occur in five tickets. The odds of having all 6 winning numbers is then (36C6)/(20C6)=2%, or 1 in 50 odds. These are not odds of winning; these are just odds of having a chance to win! Notice that 4 numbers repeat on another line.

Let's examine five tickets via random selection in another format:

54/6 Format

Line #1	5-18-28-36-43-48
#2	1-13-24-27-37-52
#3	3-21-31-44-45-49
#4	1-5-22-26-34-47
#5	3-12-19-21-24-34

Here, as in the example above, 23 different numbers are represented within our five tickets. There are, however, 54 numbers in this format. Most of the numbers don't occur. (31 of them don't occur.) The odds of having all 6 winning numbers occur in above five tickets are: (54C6)/(23C6)=0.4%, or 255 to 1 odds. We would expect to do slightly better with this format. An average of 24 numbers should occur within 5 tickets per this format; (54C6)/(24C6)=0.5%, or 192 to 1 odds of having all 6 winning numbers. Notice only one number (34) repeats on the next line.

Now let's consider a 7-number format:

40/7 Format

Line #1	3-8-16-17-18-31-36
#2	3-4-5-14-25-28-31
#3	2-7-17-19-22-29-34
#4	7-8-9-16-17-31-32
#5	3-12-17-22-24-27-32

Of the possible 40 numbers; we have 23 in our 5 tickets. This is 2 numbers more than the 21 numbers we expect to find.

repeating on next line are 100% (16.7% times 6). Thus, the following:

	New Numbers	Repeat Line 1	Repeat Line 2	Repeat Line 3	Repeat Line 4
Line 1	6	-	-	-	-
Line 2	5	1	-	-	-
Line 3	4	1	1	-	-
Line 4	3	1	1	1	
Line 5	2	1	1	1	1
Total	20	4	3	2	1

We expect 20 numbers to be represented on our 5 tickets, as per random distribution. It is, after all, random distribution, because random-creep can only function up to a saturation point. At line 7, there should be no new numbers; however, the ratio will be 22 selected numbers to 14 unselected numbers. It can only work over a few lines. Notice our 36/6 sample has 4 numbers per random creep—only one less than the 5 we expected! (5 lines times 1.00)

In 54/6 format, the odds of a number occurring are .11 (6/54). The odds of a number repeating on the next line are .66 (.11 times 6).

54/6 Format

	New	Repeat
e 1	6	-
e 2	5.34	.66
3	4.68	1.32
4	4.02	1.98
	3.36	2.64
	23.4	6.6

3.4 numbers represented is almost exactly the 24 we
er random distribution. In our 54/6 sample we only
umber repeat on the next line, but if it loses (88.9%),
wo lines!

Odds that we have all 7 winning numbers in the above 5 lines are (40C7)/(23C7)=1.3%, or about 1 in 76 odds. With the average 21 numbers, odds are (40C7)/(21C7)=0.6%, or 160 to 1 odds. Note that 6 numbers repeat on next line.

The poor distribution of numbers in random selection makes it almost impossible even to have all the winning numbers within a few lines, let alone on the same line! (Appendix I shows more examples of this—but with 40-line samples.) **And, if you don't have all winning numbers represented, you can't win!** There is a table showing how many numbers to expect on various numbers of tickets per several formats. If you don't believe my examples are representative, select your own tickets per random selection, or buy several "easy-picks" and check the results for yourself. Your results will most likely be very similar to these.

Now for an explanation of those numbers that also occur on the next line. (Shown in bold in examples.) This tendency of numbers to occur on a following line is called random repetition, and is a function of all lottery formats. There is a tabl which gives odds of a number occurring or not occurring, a that a number will repeat on a next line. Note that the odd better than 66% in almost all formats that a number will on a next line. In some formats (30/6, 33/6, 34/6, 36 40/7) we actually expect a number to repeat on a The odds of a number winning is usually less th better than 80% that it will lose!) So, what does t **means that repeating numbers are a serious l tion!** (I also call random repetition "rand "creep-factor.")

Random repetition works from one line a woven "string" of losing numbers tha throughout all number-combinations means. By itself, it can assure a very ning in any lottery format. Consider affect random number distribution a number occurring are 16.7%

Li
Li
Lin
Line
Line
Line 5
Total

The 2
expect p
had one
it defeats

In 40/7 format, the odds a number will occur are 17.5% (7/40). The odds a number will occur on the next line are 122.5% (17.5% times 7).

40/7 Format

	New	Repeat
Line 1	7	-
Line 2	5.775	1.225
Line 3	4.55	2.45
Line 4	3.325	3.675
Line 5	2.1	4.9
Total	**22.75**	**12.25**

We expect 21 numbers per random distribution. The fact that random creep has a variance shows its "short-term" range. At line 5, ratio is 20.65 selected and 19.35 numbers left. This is why I use the principle of random-creep in only line to line, and not beyond. Notice in our 40/7 sample, random creep occurs 6 times. (We expect 6.125 times. 5 lines times 1.225).

A sample of how random-creep affects results: On a 44/6 lottery, I played the following:

Line A	8-9-18-22-27-37
Line B	12-17-**20**-26-36-39
Line C	5-<u>16</u>-**20**-<u>23</u>-<u>28</u>-40

I accidentally repeated number 20 on line C. The winning numbers were 2-7-16-23-28-41. If I hadn't repeated 20, I would have had a chance at winning 4 numbers! The major factor which makes lotteries so difficult to win is the losing numbers that are assured of repeating per random selection systems. Operators are assured an unlimited supply of losing numbers to re-use. In the next chapters we will look for methods that work better than random selection.

Chapter 4

Numeric Systems and Their Limitations

When most people refer to "lottery-systems," they mean numeric systems. Origins of numeric systems are uncertain, but they have been around for hundreds of years; and have been used in lotteries held in past centuries. Most common of these numeric systems is the "wheeling system." I'm not sure where it got the name, but it might be because one number "wheels-over" in each consecutive line within the system.

There are probably more lottery "clubs" and lottery "agents" selling subscriptions per these systems than any other. Here is the usual sales pitch: They've found a "mathematical genius" with a Ph.D. from Timbuktu, who has won 20 to 30 lotteries back in his homeland; and now he is going to do the same thing in your lottery, and if you want to share in the winnings, you'd better buy a subscription.

I'd like to meet one of these "mathematical geniuses" who endorses the wheeling system (they don't return my letters), and none of the geniuses I know uses them!

A wheeling system is an effort to apply statistical sampling techniques to the selection of lottery numbers. First, select a group of numbers from the lottery format you are going to play—usually 10 to 20 numbers. After you select these numbers, you play only combinations made up of these numbers. There are four basic ways these combinations are made. Let's make a sample: In 40/6 lottery we select 12 numbers: 4, 7, 10, 12, 14, 17, 21, 26, 28, 32, 34, 38.

Standard Way

Play every possible combination that can be made from the 12 numbers. That's (12C6)=924 possible combinations: 1. 4-7-10-12-14-17; 2. 2-7-10-12-14-21; through...924. 21-26-28-32-34-38. That's 924 lottery tickets to do this.

Key Number

Make one number a "key-number" and play all possible combinations with it. The key number is played in every line. Let's make 12 the key number, so we have: 1. 12-4-7-10-14-17 through...462. 12-26-28-32-34-38. We still have 462 lottery tickets! (And, how about those combinations we didn't play?)

Groups

Break numbers down into groups, and play one number in each group with all possible combinations from other groups. Put our 12 numbers into 6 groups of 2: Group 1=4, 7. Group 2=10, 12. Group 3=14, 17. Group 4=21, 26. Group 5=28, 32. Group 6=34,38. We have: 1. 4-10-14-21-28-34 through...64. 7-12-17-26-32-38. Well, we are down to 64 lottery tickets. (But, how about all those combinations we didn't play?)

Key-Number & Group

Play a key number, and one number from each group. Key number=7. Group 2=4, 10, 12. Others same as above. We have: 1. 7-4-14-21-28-34; 2. 7-4-14-21-28-38 through...48. 7-12-17-26-32-38. Now we are down to only 48 lottery tickets. Please note: these numbers of tickets only apply to 12 numbers used in a 6-number lottery. There will be different numbers of tickets if other than 12 numbers are selected, or if the format is a 5- or a 7-number lottery. Either way, it seems like a lot of lottery tickets to buy! Numeric systems are usually used by clubs and lottery syndicates because of the expense required to play them. they can generally claim to have "a good winning percentage" because they have bought enough tickets to have acquired some winners. (If you sell and distribute a few hundred thousand, or a million tickets per year, you better have a few winners!)

Do numeric systems really improve the odds of winning? We have 924 possible combinations in the 12-number system above. The odds of having all 6 winning numbers within a selection of 12 numbers per 40/6 lottery is: (40C6)/(12C6)=4154.09 to 1. 924 possible combinations times 4154.09 to 1 odds equals 3,838,380 to 1 overall odds of winning Random (40C6) is also 3,838,380 to 1. **Numeric systems have the same overall odds as random selection.** This is true for all numeric systems. After all, the numbers we select are only a portion of the total format. The odds of the numbers times the odds of the remaining numbers will always equal the odds of the total format. Remember, numeric systems are really no more than a sampling technique. They can work if you have all the winning numbers and play all the possible combinations. Consider the following sample: We will play a 12-number numeric system. Let's use a 42/6 format. We select our 12 numbers: 1,2,7,11,12,15,20,24,28,31,37, and 42. Odds in 42/6 lottery are (42C6)=5,245,786 to 1. Odds we have all 6 winning numbers within our 12-number sample are (42C6)/(12C6)=5,677.25 to 1.

Suppose we "beat the odds" and have all 6 winning numbers in our 12-number sample. Winning numbers are: 2-7-12-20-24-31. If we played this numeric system the standard way, and played all 924 possible combinations: We have:

(1) One jackpot winner (All 6 numbers!)
(6) 5/6 winners (5 numbers—6C5=6)
(15) 4/6 winners (4 numbers—6C4=15)

Key-number (key number is #1); we play 462 tickets, and have:

No jackpot winner! (Key-number loses)

(6) 5/6 winners. (6C5=6)

(15) 4/6 winners. (6C4=15)

Group method, grouped as follows:

1,2/7,11/12,15/20,24/28,31/37,42. In 64 tickets we have:

No jackpot winner!

(4) 5/6 winners:	1)	2-7-12-20-31-37
	2)	2-7-12-24-31-37
	3)	2-7-12-20-31-42
	4)	2-7-12-24-31-42
(8) 4/6 winners:	1)	1-7-12-20-31-37
	2)	1-7-12-20-31-42
	3)	1-7-12-24-31-37
	4)	1-7-12-24-31-42
	5)	2-7-12-20-28-37
	6)	2-7-12-20-28-42
	7)	2-7-12-24-28-37
	8)	2-7-12-24-28-42

Key-number and group; key number=1; grouped as follows:
key=1/2,7,11/12,15/20,24/28,31/37,42.

In 48 tickets we have:

No jackpot winner!

No 5/6 winners! (All tickets have #1, and either 37 or 42)

(8)4/6 winners:	1)	1-2-12-20-31-37
	2)	1-7-12-20-31-37
	3)	1-2-12-20-31-42
	4)	1-7-12-20-31-42
	5)	1-2-12-24-31-37
	6)	1-7-12-24-31-37
	7)	1-2-12-24-31-42
	8)	1-7-12-24-31-42

None of the other 40 tickets have more than 3 winning numbers. and, remember—**we first had to beat 5,677 to 1 odds to get those 6 winning numbers! And, now that we have them, we must play all 924 possible combinations to assure that we win the jackpot.** Note: 924 times 5,677.25=5,245,786. (42C6)=5,245,786!! There is no overall advantage in numeric systems. They can work IF: A) You have all winning numbers within selection, and play the standard system. (All numbers) B) Have all winning numbers, and key number is winning number. C) Have all winning numbers, and one winning number within each group. D) Have all winning numbers, and key number(s), and one winning number within each group. **Even if you have all winning numbers in your selection, you must meet one of these requirements to win jackpot!**

Notice that only one number changes from line to line in numeric systems. Creep-factor affects all but one number on each line. **If you want to see losing numbers repeating, look at numeric systems!** In the next chapter we will see ways to optimize distribution of numbers and to eliminate "creep-factor," thereby improving odds of winning.

Chapter

5

Methods that Improve Odds!

As I sit here writing this book, I realize this is the first chapter most of you will read. You believe this is where the answer is? I am certain the information in this chapter will help more of you win lottery jackpots. After reading this chapter, go back and read the first four chapters; they are the foundation upon which these methods are based and will enhance your understanding of these methods.

In review, we have looked at the language of lotteries; at the concept of combinations (nCr)—the foundation upon which lotteries are based. We have looked at the ways in which most of you select your lottery numbers, and at numeric systems—and why none of these are any better than random. The two major reasons none of these "methods" are better than random are short-term random distribution and "creep-factor." Any method to reduce odds must have some control over short-term random distribution and "creep-factor."

The method to overcome the effects of random distribution and eliminate "creep-factor" is called the Matrix Method. We will look at samples of Matrix compared to Random in several formats to compare differences. Let's start by playing 5-tickets in a 33/6 Lottery:

Line	Matrix	Line	Random
1	4-17-25-26-27-28	1	3-9-11-13-28-30
2	1-6-16-20-22-32	2	8-**14**-18-**22**-23-**24**
3	2-8-9-11-23-29	3	14-16-**22**-**24**-29-32
4	10-13-14-21-31-33	4	2-8-10-**14**-**15**-**22**
5	3-5-7-15-19-30	5	3-**15**-16-19-24-28

Which set of 5-tickets offers better odds of winning? the odds are not the same for each set of tickets! There are some important differences:

	Matrix	Random
Total numbers represented:	30	19
Numbers not occurring:	3	14
Probability all winning numbers are represented:	90.9%	2.45%
Numbers that repeat—next line:	0	6
Repeat numbers—Total	0	11

There are 33 possible numbers in 33/6 format. Of 33 possible numbers; 30 *different* numbers occur in Matrix; only 19 *different* numbers occur per random distribution. All winning numbers will occur in Matrix unless 12,18, or 24 is among winning numbers. Random will not have all winning numbers if any of these—1,4,5,6,7,12,17,20,21,25,26,27,31,33—is among the winning numbers. Calculations for all winning numbers are:

Matrix: 30/33=90.9% (Simple division applies if result is greater than 90%.)*

Random: (19C6)/(33C6)=2.45% Divide by combinations if result less than 90%.

---

*The reason for this lies in mathematical theory, which is beyond the scope of this book and which is a subject for future doctoral dissertations. At somewhere between 85% and 90% in a 33/6 format, the method of calculation changes from combination to simple division.

The Matrix sample is 37 times more likely to have all winning numbers than the random sample—(90.9/2.45)=37. Our 5-ticket random sample above contains 19 different numbers. On average, five tickets in 33/6 format should have 20 differ- ?ent numbers, so this additional number raises the average probability of having all winning numbers to 3.5%—(20C6)/(33C6)=3.5%. On average, Matrix will have 26 times better odds of including all winning numbers than random per five tickets.

Consider that the average lottery bet is five dollars. In 33/6 format, this means that only one in every 28.5 lottery players has a *chance* to win by having all winning numbers among the five tickets. Until now, tickets were purchased at random odds; only 3.5% had a chance to win; now 91% have a chance! (Please Note: These odds apply only to 33/6 format and 5-ticket purchase. Odds change if format or number of tickets change.)

Let's take a look at another popular format: 44/6, but use a 7-ticket bet. Note the use of seven tickets here rather than 5-tickets. This is to use as many of the 44 numbers as possible. (7 times 6=42; 2 numbers are not used in this matrix.):

Line	Matrix	Line	Random
1	7-8-14-18-23-34	1	7-22-27-28-38-40
2	4-6-12-19-29-37	2	16-23-24-29-**34**-37
3	5-10-11-16-21-43	3	1-7-**13-34**-35-**36**
4	3-13-28-32-36-41	4	5-11-**13**-28-30-**36**
5	9-22-25-27-31-33	5	2-4-19-21-39-44
6	2-17-26-35-38-42	6	5-14-17-23-25-38
7	1-15-24-30-39-44	7	1-4-9-11-13-43

In Matrix; 42 of 44 numbers are represented. random has 30 of 44 numbers represented. Numbers 20 and 40 don't occur in matrix; numbers 3,6,8,10,12,15,18,20,26,31,32,33,41, and 42 don't occur in random. Here are the facts:

	Matrix	Random
Total numbers represented:	42	30
Numbers not occurring:	2	14
Probability all winning numbers are represented:	95.4%	8.4%
Numbers repeat—next line:	0	3
Numbers repeat—Total	0	12
Average numbers expected to occur:	42	25*

*44/6 format—7-tickets random.

The 30 numbers represented in the random sample are more than the average of 25 we expected; but there is still only an 8.4% probability that all winning numbers are present $(30C6)/(44C6)=8.4\%$. The odds are 11 times better with Matrix. Notice that the average odds (25 numbers present) per random offers only a 2.5% probability of all winning numbers being present. Matrix is 38.2 times better than this average. Even with 7-ticket bets, only one player in 40 has a *chance* to win per random selection. (Has all winning numbers.) With the average 5-ticket bet, only about 1% of players have a chance to win! This is shown as follows: $(22C6)/(44C6)=.010569833$ (just over 1%, there is an average of 22 numbers expected in a 44/6 format, 5-tickets sale.) In 44/6 format only 1 in 94 players will have all winning numbers represented per 5-ticket random bets! With a 5-ticket matrix: one in 12 players will have all winning numbers represented! Thus, with matrix, at least one in 12 players will have chance to win, rather than only one player in 94 as per random! Note: See Tables for odds of having all winning numbers per multiple-line bets for most formats, both random and Matrix.

Here's what the average 5-ticket bet looks like in 44/6:

	Matrix	Random
Total numbers represented:	30	22
Numbers not occurring:	14	22
Probability all winning numbers:	8.4%	1.1%
Numbers repeat—next line:	0	4
Numbers repeat—total:	0	8
Odds of having a chance to win:	1 in 12	1 in 94

Those of you who play 44/6 formats, using random selection (everything other than Matrix is random!) have only 1 in 94 odds of *having a chance* to win. Remember—you can't win unless you have all the winning numbers!

Now, let's see how this works with a really big lottery: 54/6 format:

Line	Matrix	Line	Random
1	1-5-15-24-28-44	1	5-18-28-36-43-48
2	3-4-17-46-48-49	2	1-13-24-27-37-52
3	11-12-13-16-21-47	3	3-21-31-44-45-49
4	25-27-31-41-42-45	4	1-5-12-26-34-47
5	2-10-34-50-52-54	5	3-19-21-24-26-34
6	8-19-23-30-37-39	6	2-3-20-22-31-53
7	9-14-20-33-38-40	7	6-11-19-34-44-54
8	6-18-26-29-43-53	8	3-4-15-20-31-33
9	7-22-32-35-36-51	9	4-11-17-25-34-38

Matrix selection has each of the 54 numbers. We expect random selection per this 54/6 format and nine lines to have 36 different numbers—exactly what we have here.

	Matrix	Random
Total number represented:	54	36
Numbers not occurring:	0	18
Probability all winning numbers:	100%	7.5%
Numbers repeat—next line:	0	4*
Repeat numbers—Total	0	18
Odds of having all winning numbers	Certain	1 in 13.3

*On average: expect 6 numbers to repeat on next line.

Some states using 54/6 format sell tickets @ 2 for a dollar. At that rate, 9-tickets are a $4.50 bet. Save $.50, and improve your odds over 13 times. Note: expanding Matrix beyond 9 lines will only hurt your odds—see Chapter 7.

If tickets are a dollar each, the average $5.00 bet looks like this:

54/6 Format—5 tickets	Matrix	Random
Total numbers represented:	30	24
Numbers not occurring:	24	30
Probability all winning numbers:	2.3%	0.5%
Number repeat—next line	0	3
Repeat numbers—Total:	0	6
Odds all winning numbers:	1 in 43.5	1 in 200

Only one of every 200 placing a 5-ticket bet, at random odds, will have all 6 winning-numbers—and a chance to win!

A number of states have gotten together on a single lottery called "Lotto-America," using 54/6 format.*

Lotto America once used a 40/7 Format (Still used in some lotteries) with random odds of 18,643,560 to 1. A 5-ticket bet looks like this:

Line	Matrix	Line	Random
1	2-7-14-15-16-23-29	1	3-**7**-**14**-16-22-28-**34**
2	4-30-34-36-37-38-40	2	**7**-9-13-**14**-**34**-35-**37**
3	12-20-21-26-31-33-35	3	4-8-10-**14**-17-**37**-40
4	1-3-6-9-11-17-24	4	6-11-13-21-22-23-26
5	5-13-18-19-25-32-39	5	1-4-5-**7**-15-16-33

A 5-ticket, random-odds bet in this format should average 24 different numbers. Our sample did one number better:

	Matrix	Random
Total numbers represented:	35	25
Numbers not occurring:	5	15
Probability all winning numbers:	36%	2.6%
Numbers repeat—next line:	0	4
Repeat numbers—Total:	0	10
Odds all winning numbers:	1 in 2.8	1 in 38.4

There is a 64% probability that one of the 5 numbers not included in our matrix will be one of the winning numbers.

*note: Lotto America has recently changed to a 45/6 "Multiple-Draw" format. See Supplement One on Multiple-Draw Lotteries and "Powerball"

(There are 7 winning numbers in this format.) There is a 97.4% probability one of the 15 numbers not included in random selection will be a winning number. On average, we expect the following on a 5-ticket bet per this format:

	Matrix	Random
Total numbers represented:	35	24
Numbers not occurring:	5	16
Probability all winning numbers:	36%	1.9%
Numbers repeat—next line:	0	6
Repeat numbers—total:	0	11
Odds all winning numbers:	1 in 2.8	1 in 52.6

Only one lottery player in 53 can expect to have all winning numbers within an average 5-ticket bet! Notice how an increase in just one additional number (25 rather than 24) increases the odds in random from 1 in 53 to 1 in 38. (40C7)/(24C7)=53; and (40C7)/(25C7)=38. Odds per Matrix are that 1 in 3 lottery players will have all 7 winning numbers, or about **20 times better than random.**

There is only one way you can be certain of having all winning numbers: **Play all the numbers!** (Or, as many as Matrix will allow!) A lottery is like a jigsaw puzzle: you have a chance to solve it if you have all the pieces. Duplicate numbers in lottery are usually worth just as much as duplicate pieces are in a jigsaw puzzle. At best, they are just leftover pieces; at worst, they can prevent solution.

How about those "left-over" numbers from Matrix? Wouldn't it be better to add an additional line and include them, so we have all the numbers, and therefore 100% probability of all winning numbers? the answer is NO! NO! NO! (That's right—3 "no's.") Let's take a look at 33/6 format:

	5-line Matrix	6-line "Matrix"
Total numbers:	30	36
Numbers represented:	30	33
Numbers not occurring:	3	0
Probability all winning numbers:	90.9%	100%

Numbers repeat—next line:	0	0 to 3
Repeat numbers—total:	0	3

Adding a sixth line improves the probability of having all winning numbers by 9.1%; but if one of these duplicated numbers loses, it defeats two lines. If all three of these duplicated numbers lose, they can defeat all six lines! Duplicate numbers hurt more than they help! Duplicate numbers are the reason random selection doesn't work! Duplicate numbers have no place in Matrix. Matrix will have exactly the same amount of numbers as format, or fewer. Some formats lend themselves to having all numbers in the Matrix: 35/5; 40/5; 30/6; 36/6; 42/6; 48/6; 54/6. All other formats will have numbers that do not occur in the matrix. (See Chapter 7 for more on this.)

Here's what happens if we expand a 7-line Matrix into an 8-line "matrix" in 44/6 format:

	7-line Matrix	8-line "Matrix"
Numbers represented:	42	44
Numbers not occurring:	2	0
Probability all winning numbers:	95.4%	100%
Numbers repeat—next line:	0	0 to 4
Repeat numbers—total:	0	4

At best, those 4 duplicated numbers will occur on two consecutive lines, and only defeat these two lines. At worst, all duplicate numbers can lose and spread across all eight lines, thereby defeating all lines. Expand 40/7 matrix to 6-lines:

	5-line Matrix	6-line "Matrix"
Numbers represented:	35	42
Numbers not occurring:	5	0
Probability all winning numbers:	36%	100%
Numbers repeat—next line:	0	0 to 2
Repeat numbers—total:	0	2

If one repeat number loses, two lines are gone. If both lose, as many as 4 lines lose.

If tickets are $.50 in 54/6 format, we have:

	$4.00 8-line Matrix	$4.50 9-line Matrix	$5.00 10-line "Matrix"
Numbers represented:	48	54	54
Numbers not occurring:	6	0	0
Probability all winning numbers:	47.5%	100%	100%
Repeat—next line:	0	0	0 to 6
Repeat—total	0	0	6

Some bargain that tenth ticket is! Those 6 duplicate numbers can defeat all 10 lines! (They're duplicates; there are at least 2 of each of them—total of 12.) If half of them win (odds are 1 in 157,779), the 3 that lose defeat from 2 to 6 lines. That one extra ticket is "poison"; it doesn't give you any numbers you don't already have (doesn't add anything to matrix); but is certain to defeat part of your matrix. If at least 5 numbers lose (there is a 67% probability that one of these duplicate numbers will win,) it is more than likely they will defeat 4 or more lines. They could defeat every line within the matrix.

All lottery formats are similar to the examples in this chapter. Their odds can be found in the tables. The rules you find here apply to all of them; there are no exceptions.

I've shown you how to get all the numbers. Now I know you're wondering about how to get them all on the same line? I've got some ideas about that in the next chapter; but first, you've got to get to this level to have any chance to win. Matrix solves this problem. It will increase 2nd and 3rd place winners also. Matrix provides the best ratio of winning numbers to losing numbers. **You can't win the jackpot without all the winning numbers!** Now, how to select numbers.

Chapter

6

How to Select Numbers

In the last chapter we looked at ways to improve the odds of having all the winning numbers. That was the easy part. Now that we are reasonably sure of having enough of the winning numbers to have a chance to win, we must find a way to get enough of them on the same line to win! This is the hard part. If there were a sure-fire way to do this, it would completely remove the element of chance from lotteries.

Here is the place for those of you who want to use "Aunt Lucy's Birthday," "The Great Zippy Zolton," or "Historical Systems." Use these "systems" on one or two lines within a matrix—just so you don't repeat any of the numbers! Of course, you are limited to using these "systems" only once within a matrix. As their numbers can be used only once, other lines within matrix will be made up of the remaining numbers of the format. Now, when none of your birthdays, "lucky-numbers," etc., is among the winning numbers, you will find the winning numbers bunched up on two or three lines within the matrix. Maybe they will all be bunched up on the same line! That is what we're looking for, isn't it?

States select winning numbers by random means. I favor this method for arranging numbers within a matrix. (Note: this is not random selection of numbers; we have already selected numbers by the use of Matrix.) We are looking at ways to randomly arrange the numbers within the matrix. Following are several ways to arrange numbers randomly:

Bingo-Lottery

Use bingo-numbers, numbered cards, numbered poker chips, numbered popsicle sticks, etc. to select lottery numbers. If you are playing a 36/6 lottery, put bingo numbers 1 thru 36 in a container. (37 thru 75 are not used here.) If you are playing 53/6 lottery, put numbers 1 thru 53 in a container. For other formats, use only those numbers used in the particular format you are playing. Now, from the container, remove numbers to be used on the first line of your matrix. **Do not replace these numbers.** Now select numbers for the second row of your matrix. **Do not replace these numbers.** Now select numbers for the third row of your matrix. Continue until you have filled as many lines as you intend to play; or until there are not enough numbers left to fill a line. **Do not play these left-over numbers in this matrix!** If it is necessary to re-use any numbers to fill a line, don't play that line. If you wish to play more tickets, put the numbers back in the container, and start another matrix. **Do not re-use, or repeat any numbers within a matrix, as this defeats the purpose of Matrix.** (That no losing number defeats more than one line.)

Using dice to select numbers

There are two types of dice we can use to select our numbers: Regular dice with six sides; and percentage dice with 10 sides. Percentage dice have 10 sides, and numbers from 0 to 9. A pair of percentage dice can give you numbers from 00 to 99. Three of these can produce numbers from 000 to 999. Odds of each number are the same with percentage dice. Regular dice offer a problem: a pair will give numbers 2 thru 12, and odds for these numbers is not the same. but there is a way a pair of regular dice can be used to represent numbers 1 thru 59, all at equal odds. first, roll a single die to determine the "tens" digit.

Like this:	Number on die	Number
	1	less than 10
	2	less than 20
	3	twenty something
	4	thirty something
	5	forty something
	6	fifty something

Roll this first die to determine the "tens" digit. To complete the rest of lottery number, two dice are needed. Preferably, dice should be of different colors or have some way of telling them apart.

DIE # 1

		1-2-3	4-5-6
	1	0	1
	2	2	3
DIE # 2	3	4	5
	4	6	7
	5	8	9
	6	roll-again	

Example: Roll the first die-4=thirty something. roll both dice: die #1=3, die #2=1. Number=0. So you first lottery number is 30. For the second number: roll the first die=3=twenty something. Roll both dice: die #1=5, die #2=4. Number=7. So the second lottery number is 27. Do this over until the first line is filled. Repeat for the second line, etc.

If you come up with a number a second time, ignore it and roll again. Continue until you have filled all lines of your matrix, or completed as many lines as you intend to play.

With percentage dice it is much the same. Dice should be different colors, so one represents "tens" and the other represents ones. (One percentage die can be used by rolling it twice.) Keep rolling over and over until one line is filled, go on to next line, etc. until matrix is complete, or desired number of lines is filled. Ignore numbers not in matrix (75, 99, etc.), and repeat numbers, and roll again. Percentage dice can produce a lot of unless numbers in some formats. In 30/6 format, most of numbers produced will be useless because they will be larger than 30, and not used in format. Use one regular die, and one percentage die. Roll both: the regular die="tens," the percentage die="ones." for example: regular die=1, percentage die=5; so the number is 05, or five. (Remember, subtract one from regular die and multiply by 10; then add number from the percentage die.) this should work best for most formats—numbers range from 00 to 59; so most numbers are usable. As elsewhere, ignore unusable and duplicate numbers and roll again.

Rubik's cubes as lottery number generators:

That's right! Cubes can be used to generate lottery numbers. (And much more efficiently than random!) the small "pocket cube" (2x2x2) has four squares on each face, so it can have 4 times 6=24 numbers. This is fewer than most lotteries; however, if you are going to play less than 4 lines and know which 24 numbers you want to play, it will work. The standard (3x3x3) cube has 9 squares per face. It can represent as many as 54 numbers (9 squares times 6 faces=54 numbers) The big "super-cube" (4x4x4) has 16 squares on each of its 6 faces. 16 squares times 6 faces=96 numbers. 96 numbers are more than needed for almost all formats; however, just don't use any numbers twice in your matrix!

Here's how to do it. Place the numbers on a cube in a random fashion. Small stick-on labels work well for this; so does tape. Apply the numbers, close your eyes and twist the cube several times. Make up your mind ahead of time which squares are going to represent which lines in your matrix. For example: each line will be the top 6 numbers on each face; or the left six numbers, etc. Notice that numbers generated with cubes are not completely random. Numbers on 3 sides of a corner square cannot be on the same line (unless you designate them as such); the same goes for numbers on 2 sides of edge squares, and the numbers on center squares. The geometry of a cube is such that they can never be on the same face. From time to time numbers should be removed and randomly re-applied. As in other cases, don't repeat any numbers. The fact is: using a cube can improve your odds of winning a lottery over using random selection!

Computers and Calculators

Most home computers can be programmed to select random numbers for your particular format. Some can even be programmed to choose numbers and arrange them into a matrix without repeating numbers. Many of the spreadsheets and software sold for various computers are also capable of generating a complete matrix in a desired format—without duplicating any numbers. Many programmable pocket computers can also be programmed to generate a complete matrix. If not, they can still be used like a calculator to generate numbers. You will just have to ignore unusable and duplicate numbers, and select again. (The key used to generate random numbers on most calculators is labeled "RND." The number generated is usually a decimal followed by 3 digits. We use the last two digits to indicate numbers, and the first digit to indicate line numbers.)

There are two basic ways I use a calculator to generate my Matrix numbers. I'll lead you through them. First, on a sheet of paper list the numbers of the lines you are going to play. Let's say five lines. Hit the "RND" button on your calculator to generate a random number. .685 comes up. Since our format is 44/6, and 85 is useless, ignore it and generate another number. .411 comes up. Write 11 on the first line. .730 comes up. Write 30 on second line, and so on until all lines are filled. When finished, you have a 5-line matrix. Put numbers in order, and check for duplicates. If there are duplicates, remove and replace with unused numbers.

The second way I sometimes use a calculator to select numbers is: On a sheet of paper, write the number of the lines you are going to play. Hit the "RND" key. Number is .617. We ignore it, as 7 is larger than the 5 lines we are playing. Try again. .195 comes up. This means number selected goes on line #5. Hit "RND" again. .507 comes up. Write "7" on line 5. Continue until all lines are filled. Put in order. Check for duplicate numbers, and replace if there are any.

Another way that is somewhat faster: Write the numbers of the lines you are going to play. In this case, make it seven. Hit the "RND" key to choose a starting number. .498 comes up. Ignore it as 98 is greater than the 44 numbers in our format. Hit "RND" key again. .922 comes up. We start with #22. Hit "RND" key. .213 comes up. Write 22 on line 3. Now we will continue with numbers in sequence using the "RND" function simply to select their line location. Go on to #23. Hit "RND" key. .919 comes up. 9 is greater than 7 lines we are playing. Start a list of unused numbers somewhere on your sheet of paper, and put 23 on that list. (We will probably come back to it again!) Hit "RND" key. .653 comes up. Write 24 on line 3. Hit "RND" key. .029 comes up. Add 25 to unused number list under 23. (9 is greater than 7-lines we are playing.) Hit "RND" key. .394 comes up. Write 26 on line number 4. Continue in sequence to the end of the matrix, in this case #44. after #44, start with #1, after #21 start again with numbers on the unused number list. Keep going until all 7 lines are filled. Put in order, check for duplicates, count unused numbers. (There should be only 2 numbers left, as 42 of the 44 numbers are used in 7 lines.) These are ways I use a calculator to generate my lottery numbers. You can use these, or create your own ways to generate numbers.

Bet Slips

Fill in bet slips directly. Choose the number of tickets you are going to play, and mark off this many spaces. Now go back and fill in the numbers, checking all other tickets within the matrix to see if this number is selected on another line. If it is, select another number and recheck. Do this until your matrix is filled, or you have filled all lines you intend to play. This may take a bit of practice—it's difficult to fill in several lines on a bet slip without duplicating numbers. You will get better at this with practice. When you get your printed tickets and see duplicated numbers, you'll do better next time. (Some states allow you to cancel tickets, and start over!)

Lotto darts

A doctor I know has made a standard five dollar "easy-pick" bet for several years—without even a 4-number winner. When I told him about these methods, he painted the dartboard in his office with the lottery numbers. Now he throws 12 darts at the board twice to fill four lines with matrix numbers. He has had two 4/6 winners within the past year, saves a dollar on each lottery he plays (4 tickets instead of 5), and has improved at darts. I can't really take credit for this, but if I hadn't told him, he'd most likely still be playing five dollars worth of "easy-picks." Anyway, he has contributed another way to selecting lottery numbers. You may arrange the numbers any way you want within a matrix. Just as long as you don't repeat numbers, you've improved your odds of winning!

Here's how those 4 ways to improve efficiency and quality (Recommended by U.S. Chamber of Commerce) relate to lotteries:

Way to Improve	Applied to Lottery
1. Try Harder:	Buy more "easy-pick" tickets.
2. Emulate:	Choose your own numbers.
3. Leapfrog:	Use numeric systems. (Leapfrog if all winning numbers are in sampling of numbers.)
4. Change the Rules of the Game:	Use Matrix Methods to improve odds.

Chapter

7

Can Lotteries be Fixed?

First we better define what we mean by fix: **"Any influence or manipulation that changes the outcome from the outcome which would have occurred had influence or manipulation not be used."** Most people believe this means the lottery operator somehow determines what the winning number combination is. I believe I can build a mechanism capable of selecting predetermined numbered balls, provided that only these predetermined balls are painted with magnetic ink. If I can do that, why can't lottery operators? Well, for one thing: All lottery drawings are audited by an accounting firm. Listen carefully to that statement! **"Drawings are audited."** Where in that statement do you see anything about any other phase of lottery operation being audited? Is the sale of lottery tickets audited? Are results audited to determine if winners are actual, and payouts as advertised? You are probably wondering if any of this is important. And what difference could it make?

Lottery operators win whenever the lottery is won. They get 50% or more up front, and usually more if payouts are spread out over several years. However, when no one wins and the lottery rolls over, the operator will have greater sales resulting from the appeal of a larger jackpot. Lottery operators increase revenues when sales increase—as a result of roll-overs. A lottery operator would have little to gain by trying to control the drawing of winning numbers. The lottery operator doesn't care who wins the lottery. In fact, they prefer that no one wins, as that increases sales and "profits" in the next drawing. Most lotteries generate the majority of their revenues as result of these "windfall" sales resulting from roll-overs.

Can the operator have any influence on the outcome of a lottery drawing? Remember that little 6/3 lottery we used back in Chapter 2? Since we used it to fund our company picnic, we wanted to make as much money with it as possible. We set up a PC to create tickets for our lotteries. There are only 20 possible number combinations in this format. The computer was to select numbers on a random basis; however, I set it up to issue everyone the same number combination. With 20 to 1 odds, I thought it unlikely that that one number combination would come up. It did! On the very first drawing, all 11 who bought tickets shared a $5.50 jackpot. they were a bit irate about it—even thought we had cheated.

The fact remains: they all had 1 chance in 20 of winning. They were just angry that they all shared the very same chance of winning. After that, they didn't allow me to program the computer any more. Our next program to control the probability of roll-over wasn't quite as good. We were able, however, to "control" the probability of roll-over to following extent:

Drawing	Total Numbers	Numbers Sold	P. of Roll-Over
First	20	10 (5)	75%
Second	20	20 (8)	60%
Third	20	40 (12)	40%
Fourth	20	50 (15)	25%

Note: Numbers in () are number-combinations sold.

After we sold 5 number-combinations, we just continued to sell these over and over in the first drawing. Since only 5 number-combinations have been sold, there is a 75% chance no one will win—and we will sell 20 tickets for the next drawing.

Then, only 8 of the 20 number-combinations will be sold—thus a 60% chance this drawing will also roll over. Then we sell 40 tickets, etc. How can we do this? 90% of all tickets sold are chosen by lottery computers. If our lottery above reaches the 4th drawing, only 12 of 120 tickets will have been chosen by a buyer. 108 of 120 tickets will have been chosen by the lottery computer. Same as in the real world.

Odds in a 46/6 format are 9,366,819 to 1. (46C6=9,366,819 combinations.) Suppose we have had a string of roll-overs, and expect to sell about 70 million tickets. If we allow all 70 million tickets to be sold randomly, about 95% of the 9,366,819 99.94 combinations, or 8.9 million combinations will be sold. Each number-combination will have been sold approximately 8 times each. At this rate, with 95% of all number-combinations being sold, the lottery is almost certain to be won. Most likely 8 winners will share the winning combination. Suppose, however, we choose to sell only 5,000,000 of the 9.4 million combinations. This gives us a 46.8% probability that the lottery will roll over. (5 million divided by 9.5 million, then subtract 1.) However, if the lottery is won, expect about 14 winners on average. (70 million tickets sold divided by 5 million combinations sold!) There are at least two ways to sell those 70,000,000 tickets:

A) 5,000,000 number-combinations times 14 tickets=70,000,000.

B) 9,000,000 number-combinations times 7.8 tickets=70,000,000.

The fact is: **There is not necessarily any correlation between the number of tickets sold and the probability of someone winning a lottery!**

It is entirely possible to write a program issuing lottery tickets that will:

A) Have winners occur at random odds.

B) Have more winners than random odds.

C) Have a greater chance of roll-over.

A basic program to sell tickets at random odds might look like this:

```
10:     Set format, Integer (1,44)
20:     Select random 6 numbers from format.
30:     Print ticket, record in memory, go to 10.
```

This program selects a line, prints and records ticket, "puts" the numbers back into pot, selects a line for next ticket, etc. this is simply selecting tickets at random odds. Let's change that program just a little:

```
10:     Set format, Integer (1,44)
20:     Select random 6 numbers from format.
30:     Print ticket, record in memory, delete numbers
        from format.
40:     Select random 6 numbers from format.
50:     Print ticket, record in memory, go to 10.
```

This program sells different numbers on two consecutive tickets. No losing number will repeat on the second line. (Yes, this is a 2-line matrix.) If all computer-chosen tickets are selected with this program, we would expect about 4 times the number of jackpot winners than per the prior program. We could extend this program up to 7-lines (42 numbers) with each number occurring once, and 95.5% probability that all winning numbers occur. Lottery operators are not about to sell an optimum "premixed ratio" of winning numbers to losing numbers with their computer chosen "easy-picks."

Now for some programs that improve the odds of roll-over. For example, we want to control a 44/6 lottery for a 50% probability of a roll-over. Possible number combinations are 44C6=7,059,052. Half (50%) of this is 3,529,526 number-combinations. If we expect to sell 20 million tickets, and know that 10% will choose their own numbers; then we know that 10% of 20 million (2,000,000) tickets will be chosen by customers. We set the counter at 3,529,526 minus 2,000,000=1,529,526. This is the number at which one computer creates only tickets based on number-combinations already issued. At this point (1,529,526) no new number-combinations are generated by computer. If we do this, the total number-combinations sold cannot exceed 1,529,526 "easy-pick" selections plus 2,000,000 buyer-selected number-combinations=a maximum of 3,529,526 number-combinations sold!

The program looks like this:

10:	Set format, integer (1,44); Counter=0.
20:	Read bet slip, if computer generated go to 40.
30:	Print ticket, record in memory, add 1 to counter, go to 20.
40:	If counter greater than 1,529,526, go to 60.
50:	Select 6 random numbers from format. Print ticket, record in memory, add 1 to counter, go to 20.
60:	Randomly select ticket from memory, duplicate numbers onto new ticket, print ticket, record in memory, add 1 to counter, go to 20.

When the drawing is conducted, 3,529,526 of the possible 7,059,052 number-combinations have been sold (although 20,000,000 tickets have been sold); therefore, the probability of roll-over is 50%. If the lottery is won, we should expect about 5 or 6 winners, as each combination that is sold has been sold an average of 5.7 times!

It is also possible to increase the odds of roll-over by improving upon the rate of random-creep. We can easily change the program which selects "easy-pick" numbers to increase the rate at which numbers repeat on the next line, thereby increasing the rate at which losing numbers occur. A random switch on line 40 generates by random a number from 1 to 5. If that random number is 1, a number is intentionally duplicated from the previous ticket. If that random number is 2 through 5, the entire ticket is selected by random selection. Here is the program:

10:	Set format, Integer (1,44).
20:	Read bet slip, if computer generated go to 40.
30:	Print ticket, record in memory, go to 20.

40:	Random switch (1,5), if 1 go to 60.	
50:	Select 6 random numbers from format, print ticket, record in memory, go to 20.	
60:	Duplicate a number from previous ticket, select 5 random numbers from format, print ticket, record in memory, go to 20.	

Line 40 assures that one additional number is duplicated every fifth line. This can also be set up to duplicate an additional number every third or fourth line, etc.

Here is what duplicating first number on every 5th line does to random samples in appendix A:

DUPLICATE NUMBERS

	Random plus Program		% Increase	Add'l
	Creep	Creep		defeated
35/5	29	32	10%	2
44/6′A″	36	41	14%	2
44/6′B′	28	32	14%	1
47/6	34	39	14%	4
40/7	50	53	6%	1

Or, to better appreciate what this "program-creep" can do to random selections, consider how the number of lines not affected by random-creep is affected by program creep in appendix A:

LINES NOT AFFECTED—where we still have a chance to win. (appendix A)

	Random Creep	Program Creep	% Increase
35/5	8	6	25%
44/6′A″	4	2	50%
44/6′B′	4	3	25%
47/6	8	4	50%
40/7	4	3	25%

Just duplicating an additional number every fifth line eliminates at least 25% of our good lines (those not affected by random-creep) in appendix A. By increasing repetition of losing numbers, odds of someone winning are further reduced, thus improving chances of roll-over.

Lottery operators can, of course, only use these programs in conjunction with their computer-chosen "easy-picks." Some operators have used "computer time" as excuse to sell only "easy-picks" when they expected to sell a large number of tickets. Consider these elements of computer time: Operations requiring 1 unit of computer time are operations not requiring comparisons or using input/output devices such as reading or printing. Two units of computer time are required for comparisons without input/output devices. Five units of computer time are required for input/output devices. Comparison of computer use time per selection of lottery numbers:

Operation	Select Numbers From Memory	Generate Random	Buyer Chosen
Read Bet Slip	5	5	5
Select Numbers	1	X	X
Generate RND Nos.	X	2	X
Store in Memory	1	1	1
Print Ticket	5	5	5
Total Computer Time	12	13	11

It requires more computer time to allow the computer to select numbers than it does if buyer selects numbers! "Easy-picks" actually require more time than buyer-chosen numbers. So, what is the real reason for lottery operators trying to sell only "easy-picks"?

There are two other ways in which lottery operators try to push duplicate numbers onto customers. First is the *structure of the lottery format*, which requires duplicating some of the numbers in order to play all numbers in the format. Examples are 34/6, which requires 2 duplicated numbers if all 36 numbers are played. That is really 2 duplicate numbers occurring 2 times resulting in 4 duplicate numbers in 6 lines. 47/6 and

53/6 formats require a duplicate number. This duplicate number will most likely defeat two lines! **It is always better to leave out numbers than to duplicate numbers!** The great temptation is to buy all the numbers, including duplicates (not realizing they usually decrease odds) so all winning numbers will occur.

The other way duplicate numbers can be "pushed" onto players is by the *ticket pricing structure*. Example is a 40/6 lottery where tickets are one for a dollar, 4 for three dollars, and 7 for five dollars. Best buy is a 6-line matrix which has a 90% probability of having all winning numbers and no duplicate numbers. But, from a money viewpoint, 7-tickets for $5 seems better. 7 tickets mean 2 duplicate numbers which can lose and spread across 4 lines, leaving the buyer a chance to win on only 3 of the 7 lines.

Another illusion is the 2-for-a-dollar tickets to encourage buying that "extra" ticket. Of special interest here is 54/6 format. Best buy is the 9-line matrix. That extra ticket, with its 6 duplicate numbers, usually defeats at least 5 of your 9 lines. In 53/6 format, this gives you 7 duplicate numbers; 11 duplicate numbers 49/6 format, etc. And, they actually let you pay for these duplicate numbers that decrease your odds of winning! Your odds are actually better if you buy 8 tickets rather than ten! Special Note: I have shown you how to use Matrix method to improve odds. Operators may come up with an "easy-pick" matrix. I can program a computer to issue tickets via matrix methods and still control the odds of roll-over. Select your own numbers!

Supplement One

"Power Ball" or Multiple-Draw Lotteries.

When I Submitted this manuscript to my publisher, I believed it would be necessary to write future editions and supplements to keep pace with changes in lotteries. I'm a bit suprised that the first supplement comes before book goes to press. Lottery operators seem to consider lotteries to be the same as a voluntary tax. They must be able to sell you tickets or they don't collect their "tax". Specifically, they want to sell as many losing tickets as possible to cover pay-outs on winning tickets and maximize "tax-collections".

From time to time, we expect the lotteries of Plentyschemia, Calliphonieum, Misusetax, Muchtaxuseless, Wastaxon, etc., to change formats or use other gimmicks to renew interest. From time to time however they may do something which will require supplements or revisions to this book. Lotto America recently switched from a 54/6 format to a 45/6 format. At first glance, it looks like they have made it easier for player to win. After all, the 54/6 format has 25,827,165 to 1 odds. Whereas the 45/6 format has odds of 8,145,060 to 1. Looks like they have improved chances by about three times? Here is the catch: Five of the six winning numbers are drawn from one set of 45 numbers. The other winning number is drawn from another set of 45 numbers! Lotto America calls this "Powerball."

I bet some of you already recognize this, and know how to play it. Since the winning numbers are drawn from more than one set of numbers—In this case two—we are actually playing against a Multiple Draw Lottery. In order to win the jackpot we must win both lotteries. One number is drawn from a set of 45 numbers so it is a 45/1 lottery with 45 to 1 odds. The other five numbers are drawn from another set of 45 numbers, and it is a 45/5 lottery. The total odds of winning are (45C1) times (45C5) = 54,979,155 to 1. (45 times 1,221,759 = 54,979,155)

The solution here is to play our Matrix Method against the 45/5 lottery. (Up to nine lines. 5 times 9 = 45.) Then add a number from 1 to 45 to each line. Note that we can cover all 45 numbers of the 45/5 lottery with a nine line matrix, but there is nothing we can do about the 45/1 lottery. That other number will always be one number in 45, and there is nothing we can do to control that number. Even with a nine line matrix we have only a 45 to 1 chance of having all six winning numbers. One chance to win costs 45 times $9 = $405.00 This is better than random odds in nine lines of 462.9 to 1. On average, expect 29 different numbers to occur per 45/5 in 9 lines per random selection. thus (45C5/29C5) times 45 = 462.9 to 1 chance of having all winning numbers. The cost of one chance to win is 462.9 times $9, or $4,166. Matrix still improves our odds against the 45/5 lottery, though there is little we can do with the 45/1 lottery. We can only guess which of the 45 numbers it will be.

40-Line Samples

Following are data samples of 40 lines per various formats. Each format has several 40-line samples, each sample chosen by a different method. Each format has at least one sample per random selection, and one sample per Matrix selection. All numbers were drawn randomly, and I committed myself to use these samples no matter how much they deviated from expected norms. Note the 3rd matrix in 44/6 format 7-line matrix sample. This matrix uses 42 of the 44 numbers. Less than 5% of the time one of these 2 numbers not used will be one of the six winning numbers. Here in this matrix, *both unused numbers are winning numbers!* Well, I committed to using whatever came up. It's very unusual for both unused numbers to be winners—**but it can happen!**

In all samples, winning numbers are underlined. In random selection, numbers duplicated on following lines are **highlighted.** This natural occurrence of numbers to repeat on next line is called "Random-Repetition," "Random-Creep," or "Creep-Factor"; and is analyzed for its ability to defeat large numbers of tickets. This analysis is on the last page of this appendix.

Following the 40-line samples are number-distributions showing how many times each number occurs in the sample. Some notes and comments are included here.

A comparison of 40-line samples per various selection methods follows the number-distributions. This is to compare range of distribution per various methods. To show the wide, haphazard distribution per random selection and tighter, more "controlled" distribution of Matrix methods. Again, some notes and comments are included.

Following is a conclusion of how the uneven distribution of numbers per random selection makes this method an undesirable way of choosing numbers. **A few losing numbers occur often enough to defeat a great majority of all tickets!**

The last page of this appendix examines "random-creep": How numbers replicate on successive lines, and usually defeat both lines! After all—most of the numbers do lose! **Replication only makes them lose more!**

35/5 FORMAT in Random Selection
Winning-Numbers: 8-14-24-31-32

Line #		Line #	
1	19-22-30-<u>32</u>-34	21	**2-6-12-27-**30
2	5-7-10-<u>31</u>-35	22	**2-22-27-<u>32</u>-34**
3	3-16-**18-26-27**	23	<u>8</u>-13-**27-**30-**34**
4	**18-21-23-26-27**	24	7-<u>8</u>-16-21-26
5	6-15-**16-**28-<u>32</u>	25	4-**7-**18-27-29
6	2-13-**16-**33-34	26	<u>14</u>-16-22-29-34
7	7-20-23-27-35	27	4-7-10-<u>14</u>-22
8	3-**12-**22-<u>24</u>-26	28	2-13-17-27-28
9	6-**12-25-**28-<u>32</u>	29	1-9-22-29-<u>31</u>
10	1-10-15-**25**-<u>31</u>	30	**1-2-16-**19-<u>32</u>
11	12-18-19-20-22	31	**2-10-16-**34-35
12	<u>8</u>-17-<u>24</u>-30-35	32	**2-11-16-**17-30
13	1-<u>8</u>-9-15-20	33	1-3-4-6-<u>8</u>
14	6-17-27-<u>31</u>-**35**	34	2-5-12-19-28
15	<u>8</u>-16-<u>24</u>-28-**35**	35	<u>14</u>-16-22-23-29

16	**8-10**-18-<u>24</u>-25	36	7-<u>**14**</u>-**16**-17-20
17	**2-10-19**-26-33	37	<u>**8**</u>-10-11-33-34
18	12-**19**-21-23-**28**	38	<u>**8**</u>-**22-23**-29-35
19	3-<u>**14**</u>-<u>**24**</u>-27-**28**	39	**2**-<u>**14**</u>-16-**23**-28
20	1-9-13-19-<u>**31**</u>	40	**2**-7-20-25-<u>**31**</u>

Winning-Number	Occurrences	Position*
8	9-times	6.2.–.–.1
14	6-times	2.3.–.1.–
24	5-times	–.–.3.2.–
31	6-times	–.–.–.2.4
32	5-times	–.–.–.2.3

200 total numbers (5 times 40) divided by 35=5.71 occurrences per number. The 31 winning numbers is slightly more than 29 expected. (5 times 5.71)

* Position is not revelant here, except to help you check my results. It does not affect any probabilities,

35/5 FORMAT (in Eight) 5-Line Matrices
Winning Numbers: <u>8-14-24-31-32</u>

Matrix #1
7-12-17-21-35
1-9-16-19-25
4-<u>8</u>-11-27-<u>32</u>
2-5-15-<u>24</u>-26
3-10-20-<u>31</u>-33

Matrix #2
<u>8-14</u>-18-33-34
3-5-6-23-27
2-10-17-20-30
1-11-22-28-35
9-12-25-26-<u>31</u>

Matrix #3
5-7-<u>8</u>-18-35
6-11-16-22-25
4-9-19-23-34
1-12-13-<u>24</u>-29
3-10-20-21-30

Matrix #5
1-13-19-25-27
11-18-22-33-34
3-16-<u>24</u>-26-30
5-9-<u>14</u>-20-<u>31</u>
2-<u>8</u>-15-21-35

Matrix #6
15-20-28-34-35
4-10-21-<u>24</u>-33
9-11-16-19-29
5-18-22-25-<u>32</u>
6-17-23-26-27

Matrix #7
3-7-9-16-33
2-10-19-20-35
<u>14</u>-22-23-25-30
18-21-<u>24</u>-27-34
1-5-11-15-29

Matrix #4	Matrix #8
10-11-18-26-30	2-13-<u>14</u>-16-<u>32</u>
2-<u>8</u>-17-23-<u>32</u>	7-<u>8</u>-15-27-34
9-20-<u>24</u>-34-35	6-17-19-22-35
3-4-12-21-33	1-3-11-30-<u>31</u>
6-<u>14</u>-16-25-28	10-21-23-29-33

Winning-Number	Occurrences	Position
8	6-times	1.4.1.–.–
14	5-times	1.2.2.–.–
24	6-times	–.–.3.3.–
31	4-times	–.–.–.1.3
32	4-times	–.–.–.–.4

35/5 FORMAT in 7-Line Matrices
Winning-Numbers: <u>8</u>-<u>14</u>-<u>24</u>-<u>31</u>-<u>32</u>

Matrix #1	Matrix #4
5-<u>8</u>-13-20-33	11-22-26-28-29
4-17-18-27-<u>31</u>	4-6-12-30-<u>32</u>
7-11-12-21-<u>32</u>	19-21-<u>24</u>-<u>31</u>-33
6-<u>14</u>-22-23-28	1-5-7-27-35
9-10-25-30-34	3-20-23-25-34
3-15-19-26-29	2-9-13-15-17
1-2-16-<u>24</u>-35	<u>8</u>-10-<u>14</u>-16-18

Matrix #2	Matrix #5
<u>14</u>-15-16-22-<u>32</u>	6-12-16-<u>31</u>-<u>32</u>
6-<u>8</u>-17-27-30	10-13-20-29-30
3-21-23-<u>24</u>-<u>31</u>	5-19-21-22-30
7-18-25-28-33	9-11-27-28-33
1-9-13-26-34	7-15-25-26-35
2-5-11-20-35	3-<u>8</u>-<u>14</u>-18-<u>24</u>
4-10-12-19-29	1-2-4-17-23

Matrix #3	Matrix #6 (5-line)
13-20-21-23-33	12-15-20-25-35
6-15-<u>24</u>-25-<u>31</u>	5-10-<u>14</u>-30-34
4-12-<u>14</u>-16-27	1-9-13-23-28
5-11-17-26-28	<u>8</u>-11-16-<u>24</u>-<u>32</u>
1-<u>8</u>-18-19-<u>32</u>	2-7-26-27-<u>31</u>
2-7-10-29-34	
3-9-22-30-35	

Winning-Number	Occurrences	Position
8	6-times	2.4.–.–.–
14	6-times	1.1.4.–.–
24	6-times	–.–.2.3.1
31	6-times	–.–.–.2.4
32	6-times	–.–.–.–.6

44/6 FORMAT in Random Selection"A"
Winning-Numbers: <u>8</u>-<u>17</u>-<u>22</u>-<u>26</u>-<u>31</u>-<u>35</u>

Line #		Line #	
1	2-11-**22**-23-37-**44**	21	4-<u>8</u>-19-<u>26</u>-32-35
2	13-**22**-**31**-39-40-**44**	22	<u>8</u>-10-**22**-29-42-44
3	5-18-25-**27**-**32**-37	23	14-20-**22**-**31**-37-41
4	**2**-**13**-18-**27**-**32**-<u>35</u>	24	1-**7**-**22**-24-**31**-38
5	**2**-**13**-16-19-34-38	25	2-6-**7**-25-27-32
6	1-11-20-**<u>35</u>**-38-44	26	3-12-14-19-20-29
7	3-6-9-10-**<u>35</u>**-37	27	16-21-<u>26</u>-27-<u>**35**</u>-39
8	<u>8</u>-13-23-<u>26</u>-**31**-44	28	**28**-30-32-33-38-40
9	3-4-<u>**8**</u>-19-24-34	29	1-15-20-<u>26</u>-**28**-42
10	2-11-12-14-18-**<u>26</u>**	30	4-5-10-18-**28**-42
11	1-<u>**8**</u>-**19**-**22**-**<u>26</u>**-33	31	<u>8</u>-13-14-**19**-<u>22</u>-33
12	10-13-**19**-<u>**26**</u>-<u>**35**</u>-40	32	**9**-**19**-<u>26</u>-**31**-**37**-40
13	1-7-12-**14**-20-28	33	**6**-**9**-14-**19**-32-**37**
14	3-**14**-15-16-29-40	34	**4**-**6**-**19**-28-34-**40**
15	4-**9**-<u>26</u>-30-<u>31</u>-**34**	35	14-**19**-21-<u>**31**</u>-<u>**35**</u>-**40**

16	9-20-**34**-39-**41**-42	36	1-12-15-**19**-**35**-39
17	**18**-26-29-**35**-**38**-**41**	37	6-9-18-21-**31**-34
18	10-13-**18**-32-**38**-39	38	2-10-14-28-**31**-35
19	6-14-22-28-**31**-37	39	4-11-16-22-**33**-43
20	2-19-23-34-40-42	40	1-14-**33**-39-42-44

Winning-Number	Occurrences	Position
8	6-times	3.2.1.–.–.–
17	none	–.–.–.–.–.–
22	9-times	–.1.5.2.1.–
25,6	10-times	–.1.3.4.1.1
31	10-times	–.–.1.3.6.–
35	10-times	–.–.–.2.5.3

Notice: There is no chance to win! Number 17 does not occur on any betting line

44/6 FORMAT in Random Selection "B"
Winning-Numbers: 6-8-18-23-28-41

Line #		Line #	
1	1-13-16-20-**30**-36	21	1-4-**20**-22-30-39
2	9-27-29-**30**-34-44	22	2-12-14-21-38-41
3	6-17-**19**-22-**41**-42	23	3-**5**-16-17-32-42
4	4-**19**-23-32-34-39	24	**5**-**7**-11-33-35-36
5	5-15-**19**-21-**38**-42	25	**7**-18-27-38-40-42
6	2-**9**-**20**-30-31-**38**	26	14-19-26-37-39-41
7	6-8-**9**-**20**-28-44	27	1-11-17-20-28-42
8	6-7-19-22-24-37	28	3-21-22-29-32-44
9	5-**12**-18-20-25-27	29	**5**-19-**33**-34-35-43
10	3-4-**12**-15-36-43	30	1-**5**-15-16-24-**33**
11	1-8-**14**-31-32-37	31	**5**-8-12-39-41-42
12	1-3-**14**-20-29-35	32	9-22-35-36-**38**-43
13	4-9-18-19-**20**-33	33	7-17-24-37-**38**-41
14	1-3-21-27-**32**-**37**	34	5-11-20-**25**-32-34
15	7-12-25-**32**-36-**37**	35	12-13-**25**-**30**-35-38
16	18-22-24-28-33-42	36	3-8-10-21-28-**30**
17	3-4-11-**18**-24-28	37	2-5-7-12-**26**-38

18	13-14-**18**-23-**24**-43	38	14-16-24-**26**-34-42
19	1-**7**-9-22-26-30	39	4-10-17-**19**-23-38
20	**7**-8-17-**20**-24-42	40	1-13-**19**-25-35-43

Winning-Number	Occurrences	Position
6	3-times	3.–.–.–.–.–
8	5-times	–.5.–.–.–.–
18	6-times	1.1.3.1.–.–
23	3-times	–.–.1.1.1.–
28	5-times	–.–.–.1.3.1
41	5-times	–.–.–.–.2.3

(The above sample is recorded from 40 actual "easy-pick" lottery tickets.)

44/6 FORMAT in 5-Line Matrices
Winning-Numbers: **8**-**17**-**22**-**26**-**31**-**35**

Matrix #1
5-10-**17**-**22**-27-43
24-29-32-34-40-42
6-9-12-**26**-38-39
4-19-21-30-33-44
2-7-14-28-**35**-37

Matrix #5
20-25-33-34-38-43
2-11-15-18-**26**-36
1-4-6-**17**-21-**35**
8-10-14-**22**-28-32
5-7-12-24-39-41

Matrix #2
11-15-**17**-19-27-30
1-10-12-25-40-41
2-20-**26**-**31**-38-42
18-21-**22**-29-36-39
3-24-33-34-43-44

Matrix #6
20-28-32-39-40-41
5-6-16-**22**-27-36
2-21-24-25-**26**-**31**
2-7-9-10-18-19
1-3-**8**-12-13-30

Matrix #3
3-24-25-32-37-39
7-14-**26**-27-29-44
9-10-18-30-**31**-**35**
5-15-28-36-42-43
2-4-**8**-16-19-21

Matrix #7
10-19-**26**-29-**31**-38
2-15-24-28-33-34
5-9-11-12-**17**-25
3-20-30-36-37-44
1-7-16-23-40-41

Matrix #4	Matrix #8
1-9-16-27-30-<u>31</u>	4-9-11-21-25-36
4-20-23-24-<u>26</u>-36	3-7-12-<u>17</u>-19-39
11-15-<u>17</u>-29-32-43	1-14-15-<u>22</u>-<u>31</u>-41
2-6-7-14-21-40	2-28-29-33-34-42
3-<u>8</u>-<u>35</u>-38-42-44	5-10-30-32-38-40

Winning-Number	Occurrences	Position
8	4-times	1.1.2.–.–.–
17	6-times	–.–.3.2.1.–
22	5-times	–.–.1.4.–.–
26	6-times	–.–.3.1.2.–
31	5-times	–.–.–.1.3.2
35	4-times	–.–.1.–.1.2

44/6 FORMAT in 7-Line Matrices
Winning-Numbers: <u>8</u>-<u>17</u>-<u>22</u>-<u>26</u>-<u>31</u>-<u>35</u>

Matrix #1
<u>8</u>-<u>17</u>-18-25-34-43
14-23-24-32-37-42
6-9-13-15-27-28
10-16-<u>35</u>-36-38-44
7-19-<u>31</u>-33-39-41
3-5-21-<u>26</u>-29-40
1-11-12-20-<u>22</u>-30

Matrix #2
10-<u>17</u>-18-19-27-36
2-11-12-21-33-43
6-9-20-25-<u>35</u>-42
3-5-13-16-<u>22</u>-34
7-28-29-32-37-40
<u>8</u>-14-30-39-41-44
1-15-24-<u>26</u>-<u>31</u>-38

Matrix #3
1-6-12-<u>31</u>-37-43
4-7-15-19-32-36

Matrix #4
1-2-3-12-16-33
<u>8</u>-11-21-34-38-43
4-<u>22</u>-27-29-42-44
5-23-25-<u>26</u>-32-<u>35</u>
9-13-15-20-37-41
6-<u>17</u>-28-30-<u>31</u>-39
7-14-18-19-36-40

Matrix #5
5-18-<u>31</u>-32-36-38
1-4-7-23-<u>35</u>-37
2-<u>8</u>-15-16-34-39'
6-25-28-33-40-43
9-14-20-21-27-30
3-12-13-<u>22</u>-<u>26</u>-44
10-19-24-29-41-42

Matrix #6 (5-line)
14-15-<u>17</u>-<u>22</u>-<u>26</u>-30
4-12-19-21-25-43

5-27-30-39-40-44
2-_8_-18-29-34-41
9-13-20-23-28-42
3-11-16-_17_-25-38
10-14-21-24-33-_35_

5-20-23-28-33-40
6-9-11-16-24-41
2-_8_-10-27-29-39

Winning-Number	Occurrences	Position
8	6-times	3.3.–.–.–.–
17	5-times	–.3.1.1.–.–
22	5-times	–.1.–.2.2.–
26	5-times	–.–.–.3.2.–
31	5-times	–.–.2.1.2.–
35	5-times	–.–.1.–.2.2

47/6 FORMAT in Random Selection
Winning-Numbers: 6-9-10-17-21-22

Line #		Line #	
1	_6_-27-34-37-43-47	21	**5-16-19-26**-28-35
2	11-16-26-28-42-45	22	_6_-**12-16-20-26**-36
3	12-15-_17_-_**22**_-35-44	23	**12**-13-15-**20**-35-44
4	11-14-19-_**22**_-25-33	24	5-16-19-_21_-28-34
5	_6_-**15-18**-29-39-44	25	11-13-24-26-32-33
6	**7**-13-**15-18**-24-**26**	26	2-8-19-**23**-38-39
7	4-_6_-**7-26**-36-42	27	_17_-20-_21_-**23**-33-40
8	12-_17_-**18**-_**22**_-24-**38**	28	1-14-18-24-25-42
9	**18**-26-32-33-**38**-47	29	15-_**17**_-19-39-45-46
10	1-5-11-23-25-43	30	2-_10_-**17-25**-32-36
11	16-19-30-31-32-39	31	1-**25**-26-29-40-43
12	4-**8**-11-12-_**22**_-29	32	5-7-**18**-19-24-28
13	1-**8**-19-25-26-**35**	33	11-**18**-_**22**_-30-31-46
14	**8**-_17_-**18**-20-27-**35**	34	1-_17_-_**22**_-23-26-35
15	5-**8-18**-_21_-23-38	35	2-3-11-14-_21_-40
16	2-16-_17_-_**22**_-27-47	36	3-20-_**22**_-34-37-**43**
17	3-12-**23**-30-35-44	37	**9-10**-12-15-29-**43**
18	3-**5**-_21_-**23**-24-45	38	18-_**22**_-**23**-39-**33**-46
19	4-**5**-_21_-**23**-24-45	39	16-**20-23-31-33**-34
20	3-**5**-15-**19-26**-43	40	**20-23**-28-**31-33**-45

Winning-Number	Occurrences	Position
6	4-times	3.1.–.–.–.–
9	1-time	1.–.–.–.–.–
10	2-times	–.2.–.–.–.–
17	8-times	1.4.3.–.–.–
21	5-times	–.–.2.2.1.–
22	9-times	–.1.3.4.1.–

47/6 FORMAT in 8-Line Matrices
Winning-Numbers: 6-9-10-17-21-22
(8-line Matrix is not recommended for 47/6 format, since duplicate number usually defeats 2 lines!)
(Duplicate number in parentheses)

Matrix #1 (11)
1-8-27-33-37-47
3-5-14-19-26-40
11-13-17-22-30-46
4-7-11-20-31-39
2-10-15-23-34-41
6-16-18-28-36-43
9-21-25-32-35-44
12-24-29-38-42-45

Matrix #2 (17)
4-13-18-22-31-38
7-12-16-23-29-37
2-11-15-17-30-40
6-10-19-24-32-42
3-8-20-27-34-41
5-9-21-26-39-45
17-25-28-35-43-46
1-14-33-36-44-47

Matrix #4 (32)
5-19-20-29-32-41
3-8-12-26-36-42
4-9-11-14-28-43
10-15-18-23-27-45
1-6-21-31-35-44
2-7-13-33-37-46
16-17-24-32-39-47
22-25-30-34-38-40

Matrix #5 (39)
7-16-21-29-35-44
5-8-13-18-25-33
11-17-20-32-34-39
2-4-10-19-36-40
3-12-14-26-41-43
1-6-27-37-42-46
15-23-28-31-38-45
9-22-24-30-39-47

Matrix #3 (18)
<u>10</u>-15-19-25-33-41
3-13-18-24-30-37
4-<u>6</u>-20-32-36-38
1-8-18-23-29-47
5-7-12-28-35-42
2-<u>9</u>-16-27-31-45
11-<u>17-21</u>-34-39-43
14-<u>22</u>-26-40-44-46

Winning-Number	Occurrences	Position
6	5-times	2.3.–.–.–.–
9	5-times	2.3.–.–.–.–
10	5-times	2.2.1.–.–.–
17	6-times	1.3.1.1.–.–
21	5-times	–.1.4.–.–.–
22	5-times	1.2.–.2.–.–

40/7 FORMAT in Random Selection
Winning-Numbers: <u>5</u>-<u>9</u>-<u>20</u>-<u>22</u>-<u>37</u>-<u>39</u>-<u>40</u>

Line #		Line #	
1	10-14-17-18-**29**-**37**-40	21	2-19-21-<u>22</u>-27-32-<u>**40**</u>
2	5-6-7-9-**29**-**37**-38	22	10-12-**21**-29-31-34-<u>**40**</u>
3	9-**11**-15-20-**26**-31-34	23	11-14-17-<u>22</u>-30-38-<u>**39**</u>
4	**11**-17-19-**26**-32-35-36	24	4-10-13-24-33-**34**-<u>**39**</u>
5	9-14-16-**18**-**26**-29-40	25	7-27-30-31-**34**-38-<u>**39**</u>
6	4-**11**-13-**18**-20-**22**-23	26	1-<u>9</u>-12-14-**15**-21-40
7	4-**11**-14-17-**22**-**23**-39	27	<u>9</u>-**15**-17-**25**-28-29-39
8	<u>20</u>-24-26-**31**-33-36-**38**	28	1-3-6-7-<u>20</u>-**25**-38
9	2-7-8-19-<u>**20**</u>-**31**-38	29	14-24-26-27-31-32-**38**
10	2-3-<u>5</u>-**11**-13-34-<u>37</u>	30	<u>5</u>-7-17-18-23-29-30
11	<u>9</u>-14-19-<u>22</u>-26-33-<u>**39**</u>	31	<u>5</u>-13-<u>14</u>-15-<u>**20**</u>-33-**37**
12	1-3-4-7-<u>20</u>-23-24	32	10-12-**14**-<u>**20**</u>-**31**-**37**-38
13	8-26-**31**-32-34-**35**-<u>**39**</u>	33	2-8-**16**-24-**31**-34-37
14	13-28-29-30-**31**-**35**-36	34	11-**16**-17-20-26-33-35
15	14-18-25-26-31-37-39	35	**8**-12-14-15-22-36-37

16	5-7-8-23-34-35-37	36	1-8-11-23-29-31-32
17	3-9-11-16-23-24-28	37	2-8-11-22-29-31-32
18	5-10-14-20-24-31-37	38	2-5-7-8-11-12-31
19	5-11-12-14-19-31-34	39	15-20-21-25-27-30-37
20	2-15-26-29-31-38-39	40	2-8-9-12-17-19-28

Winning-Number	Occurrences	Position
5	8-times	6.1.1.–.–.–.–
9	8-times	4.2.1.1.–.–.–
20	11-times	1.1.–.4.5.–.–
22	7-times	–.–.–.4.2.1.–
37	11-times	–.–.–.–.–.4.7
39	9-times	–.–.–.–.–.–.9
40	5-times	–.–.–.–.–.–.5

40/7 FORMAT in 5-Line Matrices
Winning-Numbers: 5-9-20-22-37-39-40

Matrix #1
3-5-11-12-16-37-40
1-7-10-15-20-28-35
6-25-27-30-31-34-39
2-4-8-13-19-24-26
17-21-22-23-32-33-38

Matrix #2
1-3-8-13-19-25-26
10-16-18-30-34-35-40
2-7-9-11-22-29-38
4-20-23-28-31-36-39
5-6-14-24-27-32-37

Matrix #3
7-14-15-17-25-28-37
4-5-9-11-27-29-34
1-2-3-6-10-38-40
8-13-20-23-26-33-35
12-16-18-19-22-30-31

Matrix #5
16-20-22-24-30-34-35
2-4-8-25-29-38-40
6-12-13-14-18-23-31
3-5-15-26-27-28-37
1-7-9-11-17-19-21

Matrix #6
3-4-6-8-12-24-35
2-9-11-13-27-33-38
14-16-17-19-22-30-31
15-18-20-26-29-36-37
7-10-23-25-28-32-39

Matrix #7
1-10-22-27-28-29-38
4-5-12-15-19-21-31
2-17-18-20-23-25-37
3-8-13-16-32-33-34
6-7-24-35-36-39-40

Matrix #4	Matrix #8
6-8-15-16-25-38-<u>39</u>	2-<u>5</u>-14-15-23-25-29
1-<u>9</u>-11-<u>20-22</u>-28-30	1-7-<u>20</u>-27-31-35-38
18-24-29-31-33-36-<u>40</u>	3-6-8-10-17-19-26
7-10-12-19-23-32-34	<u>9</u>-11-18-21-32-33-<u>40</u>
4-13-17-26-27-35-<u>37</u>	4-<u>22</u>-24-28-34-36-<u>39</u>

Winning-Number	Occurrences	Position
5	6-times	1.5.–.–.–.–.–
9	6-times	1.2.3.–.–.–.–
20	8-times	–.2.3.2.1.–.–
22	8-times	–.1.3.–.4.–.–
37	7-times	–.–.–.–.–.1.6
39	7-times	–.–.–.–.–.1.6
40	7-times	–.–.–.–.–.–.7

Distribution

35/5 FORMAT in Random Selection

12-times	16
11-times	2
10-times	27
9-times	<u>8</u>,22
8-times	28
7-times	7,10,19,34,35
6-times	1,12,<u>14</u>,<u>31</u>
5-times	6,17,18,20,23,<u>24</u>,26,29,30,<u>32</u>
4-times	3,25
3-times	5,9,13,15,21,33
2-times	4,11
1-time	none
none	none

Notice; One losing number (16) defeats 12 tickets. 2 occurs 11 times, but 5 times in conjunction with #16; so #2 increases number of losing tickets to 18. Nine more tickets are defeated by losing numbers 27 and 22. Some distribution! Only four losing numbers defeat 27 or our 40 tickets! Only 11.4% of numbers ruin 67.5% of our tickets

Distribution

35\5 Format in 5-line Matrices

8-times	11,35
7-times	3,9,10,16,20,21,25,33,34
6-times	1,2,8,18,19,22,23,24,27,30
5-times	5,6,14,15,17,26
4-times	4,7,12,31,32
3-times	13,28,29
2-times	none
1-time	none
none	none

Notice the much tighter distribution with Matrix. No losing number can occur more than once per Matrix. Therefore, no losing number can defeat more than one line per matrix. Matrix also offers much higher probability that all winning numbers will occur than do random methods.

Distribution

35/5 Format in 7-line Matrices

5-times	3,4,6,17,18,19,21,25,29,33
6-times	All other numbers.

Please note that the 10 numbers that occur only 5 times are the "missing-numbers" from the last matrix. If the last matrix were 7-lines rather than 5-lines, these number would complete it; then, every number would occur exactly 6-times. Distribution cannot be any tighter.

Distribution

44/6 Format in Random Selection "A"

12-times	19
11-times	none
10-times	26,31,35
9-times	14,22
8-times	40
7-times	2,13,18,28,32,34,37,38
6-times	1,4,6,8,9,10,39,44
5-times	20,33,42
4-times	11,12,16,27,29
3-times	3,7,15,21,23,41
2-times	5,24,25,30,43
1-time	none
none	17,36

Although 4 of 6 most-occurring numbers are winning numbers (26,31,35,22), just 4 losing numbers (19,14,10,18) defeat 26 tickets. **Only 9% of numbers defeat 65% of our tickets!** And of course, we have no chance to win because number 17 doesn't occur.

Distribution

44/6 Format in Random Selection "B"

10-times	20
9-times	1,5,38,42
8-times	7,24
7-times	3,19,22,30,32,36
6-times	4,9,12,17,18,37
5-times	8,25,28,33,41,43
4-times	11,13,14,21,26,27,34,35,39
3-times	2,6,15,16,23,44
2-times	10,29,31
1-time	40
none	none

Note that only five losing numbers (20,1,5,38,42) defeat 30 of our 40 tickets! **11% of total numbers have ruined the chance of winning on 75% of our tickets!**

Distribution

44/6 Format in 5-line Matrices

7-times	2,10,30
6-times	1,3,4,5,9,<u>17</u>,24,25,<u>26</u>,28,29,32,36,38,39,40
5-times	12,14,15,19,20,<u>22</u>,27,<u>31</u>,33,34,41,42,43,44
4-times	6,<u>8</u>,11,16,18,21,<u>35</u>
3-times	23,37
2-times	none
1-time	13
none	none

Distribution

44/6 Format in 7-line Matrices

6-times	5,6,<u>8</u>,9,12,14,15,16,19,20,21,25,27,28, 29,30,33,39,40,41,43
5-times	1,2,3,7,10,11,13,<u>17</u>,18,<u>22</u>,23,24,<u>26</u>,<u>31</u>, 32,34,<u>35</u>,36,37,38,42,44
4-times	4

Distribution

40/7 Format in Random Selection

17-times	31
16-times	none
15-times	none
14-times	none
13-times	14
12-times	none

11-times	11,20,37
10-times	26
9-times	29,34,38,39
8-times	2,5,7,8,9,17
7-times	15,22,23,24
6-times	10,19,33
5-times	12,13,18,27,30,32,35,40
4-times	1,3,4,21,36
3-times	25,28
2-times	6
1-time	none
none	none

3 losing numbers defeat 31 lines! 7.5% of numbers defeat 77.5% of our tickets!

Distribution

40/7 Format in 5-Line Matrices

8-times	4,8,19,20,22,23,25,27,28,31,35,38
7-times	1,3,6,7,10,11,13,16,17,18,24,26,29,34,37,39,40
6-times	5,9,15,30,32,33
5-times	2,12,14,36
4-times	21
3-times	none
2-times	none
1-time	none
none	none

Analysis of distributions: 35/5 Format

Occurs	Random	5-Line Matrix	7-Line Matrix
12-times	1		
11-times	1		
10-times	1		
9-times	2		
8-times	1	2	
7-times	5	9	

6-times	4	10	25
5-times	10	6	10
4-times	2	5	
3-times	6	3	
2-times	2		
1-time	0		
none	0		

The range of distribution with random selection is 11 numbers (2 through 12). With 5-line Matrices, the range of distribution is only 6 numbers (3 through 8). More efficient 7-line Matrices have a range of distribution of only 2 numbers (5 and 6). Notice, if our sample size had been 42 lines rather than 40, all 35 numbers would have occurred exactly 6 times with 7-line Matrices; this assures that each winning number occurs in each Matrix.

Analysis of Distributions: 44/6 Format

Occurs	Random (A)	(B)	5-Line Matrix	7-Line Matrix
12-times	1			
11-times	0			
10-times	3	1		
9-times	2	4		
8-times	1	2		
7-times	7	6	3	
6-times	9	6	16	21
5-times	3	6	14	22
4-times	5	9	7	
3-times	6	6	2	
2-times	5	3	0	
1-time	0	1	1	
none	2			

Random "A": 4 losing numbers (19,14,40,18) defeat 26 of 40 tickets. Only 9% of numbers defeat 65% of tickets. Random "B": 5 losing numbers (20,1,5,38,42) defeat 30 of 40 tickets.

Only 11% of numbers defeat 75% of tickets! Notice the tighter range of distribution with Matrix methods.

Analysis of Distributions: 47/6 Format

Occurs	Random	8-Line Matrix
11-times	1	
10-times	2	
9-times	2	
8-times	4	
7-times	4	
6-times	3	5
5-times	7	42
4-times	12	
3-times	7	
2-times	3	
1-time	1	
none	1	

Please note that in random selection the five most frequently occurring numbers (26,18,23,19,22) defeat 33 of 40 total lines. **Only 10.6% of total numbers defeat 82.5% of total tickets!**

Much more even distribution results with Matrix. Note that using an 8-line matrix (48-number) in 47/6 format requires that one of the 47 numbers must repeat. **This usually defeats two lines!** (12.8% probability a number will win in this format.) For this reason, I don't recommend an 8-line matrix per this format. Note that a duplicate number won in only one of five matrices in our 40=line sample.

Analysis of Distributions: 40/7 Format

Occurs	Random	5-Line Matrix
17-times	1	
16-times	0	
15-times	0	
14-times	0	
13-times	1	

12-times	0	
11-times	3	
10-times	1	
9-times	4	
8-times	6	12
7-times	4	17
6-times	3	6
5-times	8	4
4-times	5	1
3-times	2	
2-times	1	
1-time	0	
none	0	

Random selection: only three losing numbers (31,14,11) defeat 31 of our 40 tickets. **Only 7.5% of numbers ruin 77.5% of total tickets!**

Analysis of Random Selection

Analysis of our 40-line Random selections is as follows:

Format	Losing Numbers	Tickets Defeated	Percent Numbers	Percent Tickets
35/5	4	27	11.4	67.5
44/6 "A"	4	26	9.0	65.0
44/6 "B"	5	30	11.4	75.0
47/6	5	33	10.6	82.5
40/7	3	31	7.5	77.5

In the short run of a few selections, the varied distribution of numbers, and very unlikely probability of even having all the winning numbers within a few lines, makes this an undesirable method of play. In general, about 10% of the most frequently occurring numbers lose, and in losing they defeat about 75% of all tickets.

Notice also there is no possibility of winning in sample 44/6 "A". One winning number (17) doesn't occur anywhere within 40-lines. It is not possible to win the jackpot with having all the winning numbers. *out*

Analysis of Random Repetition
("CREEP-FACTOR")

Random Sample 35/5 Format

Only 8 lines (1,2,7,11,20,28,33,34) are not affected by repeating numbers on next line. 80% of our tickets are affected by "creep-factor." On average, we expect 71.5% of tickets to be affected in this format. (14.5 times 5) In our sample we had 29 duplicated numbers, of which 7 were winning numbers. (On average, we expect only 4 of 29 duplicate numbers to be winners.) (29 times .143=4)

Random Sample "A" 44/6 Format

Only 4 lines (19,20,26,27) are not affected by "creep-factor." 90% of tickets are affected! Of 36 duplicate numbers, 10 are winning numbers. On average, we expect 81.6% of tickets to be affected in 44/6 format. (13.6 times 6=81.6%) We also expect that only 5 of 36 duplicate numbers will win. (36 times .135=5) We are well above average here! However, "creep-factor" still defeats most of our tickets!

Random Sample "B" 44/6 Format

Only 4 lines (22,26,27,28) are not affected by "creep-factor." 90% are affected, higher than the expected average of 81.6%. (13.6 times 6=81.6%) 28 numbers duplicate on the next line, and 4 are winning numbers. Exactly as expected. (28 times .136=4)

Random Sample 47/6 Format

"Creep-factor" should affect 76.8% (6 times .128) of our tickets. 80% (32 of 40) of tickets are affected. Only lines 1,2,10,11,16,24,25,28 are not affected by "random-creep." 34

numbers are duplicated by creep; 3 are winning numbers. This is close to the 3 winning numbers we predict: 34 times .128=3.

Random Sample 40/7 Format

In this format, we expect 1.225 of the 7 numbers to repeat on the next line. (.175 times 7=1.225) our sample has 50 duplicated numbers on 40 lines. 1.25 duplicated numbers per line. Only 4 lines are not affected by creep (10%): 11,12,39,40. **90% of tickets are defeated by "creep-factor."** 11 of the 50 numbers duplicated by creep are winners. This is more than the 9 winning numbers expected: 50 times .175=9.

"Creep-Factor" by itself makes random selection an undesirable method of play. Losing numbers duplicating on next line defeat most tickets in almost all formats!

Note: For graphic illustration of how "Creep Factor" affects results, take a pencil or highlighter and connect all the numbers from line to line in bold <u>that are not underlined</u> in the Random Selection Examples. **None of the tickets this line passes through has any chance of winning!** These numbers are lost to duplicating losing numbers just on the next line!

Lottery Fever

Michigan's lottery obsession finally breaks
by Detroit Free Press Staff Writers Frank Bruni and Linda
Stewart (9-15-1990)
Florida jackpot at $105 million

The wait—finally—was over Sunday; the madness had run
its course. No longer were people hocking jewelry to purchase
just a dozen more tickets.

Announced Saturday, the winning numbers for the second-
biggest lottery purse in U.S. history were 5-6-21-34-35-45. Six
tickets bear the combination, each worth an estimated $17.5
million. Winning ticket holders had to wait until lottery offices
opened today to validate the tickets, which will be paid off
over 20 years.

Many of the Florida tickets were purchased by out-of-state
residents. Several from the Detroit area, like Martha, called the
Free Press on Sunday to try to learn if their numbers were the
magic ones.

"Could you give them to me again?" Martha pleaded. Her
hushed voice carried a note of urgency.

"I'm an impoverished wife of a wealthy man," she said.

"The first thing I'm going to do is get a divorce. It's true. Everyone who knows me know it."

To see if she had won, Martha had to go through 150 tickets, each purchased at a 100-percent markup of $2 from a lottery players network in Pennsylvania to which she belongs.

Several callers said they had bought tickets at markups from scalpers, but wouldn't identify themselves for fear they or the sellers would get in trouble.

Social Programs and Taxes

PBS shows why lotteries are a gamble for the poor
by Marc Gunther, Detroit Free Press TV Writer

The booming lottery business is examined in "Betting on the Lottery," a lively and thoughtful episode of "Frontline" on PBS. Why is the lottery a symptom of our weakened political system? Because it's an easy way out for elected officials. As correspondent James Reston Jr. says: "Instead of making hard choices about social programs and taxes, we have let our politicians use the lottery to pick up the tab." The result: Last year, Americans spent $20 billion—that's right, billion—on lottery tickets. That's money that could just as easily have been saved, invested, or spent on consumer goods that create jobs and drive the economy.

Interestingly, those bettors fueling the lottery fever tend to be people who can least afford to fritter their money away on long shots. In Illinois, Reston found a Yugoslavian immigrant who toils as a janitor and has lost $70,000 on the lottery over the years. In Maryland, two-thirds of the lottery money comes from Baltimore and suburban Prince Georges County, poor and mostly black areas.

This "Frontline" is valuable because it reminds us to look again at a phenomenon that is unfolding before our eyes, as our state governments work harder and harder to turn their own citizens into losers.

Bibliography

This is not a formal bibliography, but I have read, and certainly been influenced by the following sources, and wish to give them credit:

"How to Solve Rubik's Revenge," by Jeffrey Adams, PhD, Dial Press, New York, 1982.

"The Winning Solution," by Minh Thai, Banbury Books, Pennsylvania, 1982.

"Probabilities in Everyday Life," by John D. McGervey, PhD, Ivy Books (Random House), New York, 1986.

"By Chance A Winner: The History of Lotteries," by George Sullivan, Dodd & Mead, New York, 1972.

"The Unseemly Hard Sell of Lotteries," by Charles T. Clotreltes and Philip J. Cook, New York Times, 20 Aug. 1987.

"Elementary Business Statistics," by Freund and Williams, Prentice-Hall, New Jersey, 1964.

"The Basics of Roulette," by J. Edward Allen, Cordoza Publishing, California, 1985.

The Malcolm Baldridge National Quality Award Consortium Inc. P.O. Box 442 Milwaukee, WI 53201-0443.

Detroit Free Press
321 W. Lafayette
Detroit, Mi 48226

Detroit News
615 Lafayette
Detroit, MI 48226

Lottery Players Magazine
321 New Albany Road
Moorestown, NJ 08057

Table

1

Random Distribution of Lottery Formats

8/3 Format	Numbers	Percent	Odds to One
3/3	1	5.0	20
2/3	9	45.0	2.2
1/3	9	45.0	2.2
0/3	1	5.0	20
Total	20	100.0	

8/3 Format	Numbers	Percent	Odds to One
3/3	1	1.79	56
2/3	15	26.79	3.7
1/3	30	53.56	1.87
0/3	10	17.86	5.6
Total	56	100.0	

10/3 Format	Numbers	Percent	Odds to One
3/3	1	0.83	120
2/3	21	17.5	5.7
1/3	63	52.5	1.9
0/3	35	29.2	3.4
Total	120	100.0	

35/5 Format	Numbers	Percent	Odds to One
5/5	1	0.0003	324,632
4/5	150	0.046	2,164
3/5	4,350	1.34	75
2/5	40,600	12.5	8
1/5	137,025	42.2	2.4
0/5	142,506	43.6	2.3
Total	324,632	99.99	

40/5 Format	Numbers	Percent	Odds to One
5/5	1	0.00015	658,008
4/5	175	0.027	3,760
3/5	5,950	0.90	111
2/5	65,450	9.95	10
1/5	261,800	39.79	2.5
0/5	324,632	49.34	2
Total	658,008	100.0	

30/6 Format	Numbers	Percent	Odds to One
6/6	1	0.00017	593,775
5/6	144	0.024	4,123
4/6	4,140	0.697	143
3/6	40,480	6.82	15
2/6	159,390	26.85	3.7
1/6	255,024	42.95	2.3
0/6	134,596	22.67	4.4
Total	593,775	100.0	

33/6 Format	Numbers	Percent	Odds to One
6/6	1	0.00009	1,107,568
5/6	162	0.0146	6,837
4/6	5,265	0.475	210
3/6	58,500	5.282	19
2/6	263,250	23.768	4.2
1/6	484,380	43.734	2.3
0/6	296,010	26.726	3.7
Total	1,107,568	99.99	

34/6 Format	Numbers	Percent	Odds to One
6/6	1	0.000074	1,344,904
5/6	168	0.0125	8,005
4/6	5,670	0.422	237
3/6	65,520	4.872	21
2/6	307,125	22.836	4.2
1/6	589,680	43.846	2.3
0/6	376,740	28.012	3.6
Total	1,344,904	100.0	

36/6 Format	Numbers	Percent	Odds to One
6/6	1	0.000051	1,947,792
5/6	180	0.0092	10,821
4/6	6,525	0.335	299
3/6	81,200	4.169	24
2/6	411,075	21.105	4.7
1/6	855,036	43.898	2.3
0/6	593,775	30.485	3.3
Total	**1,947,792**	**100.0**	

39/6 Format	Numbers	Percent	Odds to One
6/6	1	0.000031	3,262,623
5/6	198	0.0061	16,478
4/6	7,920	0.2427	412
3/6	109,120	3.345	30
2/6	613,800	18.881	5.3
1/6	1,424,016	43.646	2.3
0/6	1,107,568	33.947	2.9
Total	**3,262,623**	**100.0**	

40/6 Format	Numbers	Percent	Odds to One
6/6	1	0.00003	3,838,380
5/6	204	0.0053	18,816
4/6	8,415	0.22	456
3/6	119,680	3.1	32
2/6	695,640	18.1	5.5
1/6	1,669,536	43.5	2.3
0/6	1,344,904	35.0	2.8
Total	**3,838,380**	**99.99**	

42/6 Format	Numbers	Percent	Odds to One
6/6	1	0.00002	5,245,786
5/6	216	0.00041	24,286
4/6	9,450	0.18	555
3/6	142,800	2.7	36.7
2/6	883,575	16.8	36.7
1/6	2,261,952	43.1	2.3
0/6	1,947,792	37.1	2.7
Total	**5,245,786**	**99.99**	

44/6 Format	Numbers	Percent	Odds to One
6/6	1	0.000014	7,059,052
5/6	228	0.0032	30,960
4/6	10,545	0.149	669
3/6	168,720	2.39	41.8
2/6	1,107,225	15.685	6.4
1/6	3,011,652	42.66	2.3
0/6	2,760,681	39.1	2.2
Total	7,059,052	99.99	

45/6 Format	Numbers	Percent	Odds to One
6/6	1	0.000012	8,145,060
5/6	234	0.0029	34,808
4/6	11,115	0.136	733
3/6	182,780	2.224	45
2/6	1,233,765	15.147	6.6
1/6	3,454,542	42.413	2.4
0/6	3,262,623	40.056	2.5
Total	8,145,060	99.98	

46/6 Format	Numbers	Percent	Odds to One
6/6	1	0.000011	9,366,819
5/6	240	0.00256	39,028
4/6	11,700	0.1249	801
3/6	197,600	2.1096	47
2/6	1,370,850	14.635	6.8
1/6	3,948,048	42.149	2.4
0/6	3,838,380	40.978	2.44
Total	9,366,819	99.99	

47/6 Format	Numbers	Percent	Odds to One
6/6	1	0.0000093	10,737,573
5/6	246	0.00229	43,649
4/6	12,300	0.1146	873
3/6	213,200	1.986	50
2/6	1,519,050	14.147	7
1/6	4,496,388	41.875	2.4
0/6	4,496,388	41,875	2.3
Total	10,737,573	99.99	

48/6 Format	Numbers	Percent	Odds to One
6/6	1	0.0000081	12,271,512
5/6	252	0.00205	48,696
4/6	12,915	0.105	950
3/6	229,600	1.871	53
2/6	1,678,950	13.682	7.3
1/6	5,104,008	41.592	2.4
0/6	5,245,786	42.748	2.3
Total	12,271,512	100.0	

49/6 Format	Numbers	Percent	Odds to One
6/6	1	0.0000072	13,983,816
5/6	258	0.0018	54,201
4/6	13,545	0.0969	1,032
3/6	246,820	1.765	57
2/6	1,851,150	13,238	7.6
1/6	5,775,588	41.302	2.4
0/6	6,096,454	43.596	2.3
Total	13,983,816	99.99	

53/6 Format	Numbers	Percent	Odds to One
6/6	1	0.0000044	22,957,480
5/6	282	0.00123	81,410
4/6	16,215	0.0706	1,416
3/6	324,300	1.413	71
2/6	2,675,475	11.654	8.6
1/6	9,203,634	40.09	2.5
0/6	10,737,573	46.772	2.1
Total	22,957,480	100.0	

54/6 Format	Numbers	Percent	Odds to One
6/6	1	0.0000039	25,827,165
5/6	288	0.00112	89,678
4/6	16,920	0.0655	1,526
3/6	345,920	1.340	75
2/6	2,918,700	11.301	8.8
1/6	10,273,824	39.779	2.5
0/6	12,271,512	47.514	2.1
Total	25,827,165	100.0	

40/7 Format	Numbers	Percent	Odds to One
7/7	1	0.0000054	18,643,560
6/7	231	0.00124	80,708
5/7	11,088	0.0595	1,681
4/7	190,960	1.0243	98
3/7	1,432,200	7.682	13
2/7	4,984,056	26.733	3.7
1/7	7,752,976	41.585	2.4
0/7	4,272,048	22.914	4.4
Total	18,643,560	99.99	

90/5 Format	Numbers	Percent	Odds to One
5/5	1	0.0000023	43,949,268
4/5	425	0.000967	103,410
3/5	35,700	0.08123	1,231
2/5	987,700	2.247364	44.5
1/5	10,123,925	23.035480	4.3
0/5	32,801,517	74.634956	1.3
Total	43,949,268	99.999999	

30/9 Format	Numbers	Percent	Odds to One
9/9	1	0.000007	14,307,150
8/9	189	0.001	75,699
7/9	7,560	0.053	1,892
6/9	111,720	0.781	128
5/9	754,110	5.27	19
4/9	2,563,974	17.92	5.6
3/9	4,558,176	31.86	3.1
2/9	4,186,080	29.26	3.4
1/9	1,831,410	12.80	7.8
0/9	293,930	2.05	48.7
Total	14,307,150	99.99	

Table

2

Probability that Numbers Will Occur, Not Occur, Repeat on Next Line

Format	Occur	Not-Occur	Repeat on Next Line
6/3	50.0%	50.0%	150.0%
8/3	37.5	62.5	112.5
10/3	30.0	70.0	90.0
35/5	14.3	85.7	71.5
40/5	12.5	87.5	62.5
30/6	20.0	80.0	120.0
33/6	18.2	81.8	109.2
34/6	17.6	82.4	105.6
36/6	16.7	83.3	100.2
39/6	15.4	84.6	92.4
40/6	15.0	85.0	90.0
42/6	14.3	85.7	85.8
44/6	13.6	86.4	81.6
45/6	13.3	86.7	80.0
46/6	13.0	87.0	78.0
47/6	12.8	87.2	76.8
48/6	12.5	87.5	75.0
49/6	12.2	87.8	73.2
53/6	11.3	88.7	67.8
54/6	11.1	88.9	66.6
40/7	17.5	82.5	122.5
30/9	30.0	70.0	270.0
90/5	05.6	94.4	28.0

Note: All numbers are in percent.

Table

3

Average Numbers Represented:
Random vs. Matrix

Example: If you bet 5 tickets in 34/6 lottery, you can expect 20 different numbers to be represented per random selection; or 30 different numbers per Matrix selection. Free Numbers represent additional numbers selected by using Matrix.

34/6 Format

Tickets	Random	Matrix	Free Numbers
5	20	30	10
6	23	30 (5 tickets)	7
7	26	30 (5 tickets)	4
8	27	30 (5 tickets)	3
9	28	30 (5 tickets)	2

42/6 Format

Tickets	Random	Matrix	Free Numbers
5	22	30	8
6	24	36	12
7	25	42	17
8	27	42 (7 tickets)	15
9	29	42 (7 tickets)	13

48/6 Format

Tickets	Random	Matrix	Free Numbers
5	23	30	7
6	25	36	11
7	28	42	14
8	31	48	17
9	33	48 (8 tickets)	15

54/6 Format

Tickets	Random	Matrix	Free Numbers
5	24	30	6
6	28	36	8
7	30	42	12
8	34	48	14
9	36	54	18

40/5 Format

Tickets	Random	Matrix	Free Numbers
5	18	25	7
6	20	30	10
7	23	35	12
8	26	40	14
9	27	40 (8 tickets)	13
10	29	40 (8 tickets)	11

40/7 Format

Tickets	Random	Matrix	Free Numbers
4	21	28	7
5	24	35	11
6	26	35 (5 tickets)	9
7	28	35 (5 tickets)	7
8	30	35 (5 tickets)	5
9	31	35 (5 tickets)	4

Notice that Matrix method doesn't allow numbers to repeat. If numbers repeated, it would no longer be Matrix. Above table notes maximum number of tickets within Matrix.

A) Average Numbers Represented By Random Selection

	Number of Tickets Purchased								
Format	2	3	4	5	6	7	8	9	10
35/5	9	13	16	19	21	23	25	26	27
40/5	9	13	16	19	22	24	26	28	30

30/6	11	15	18	20	22	24	25	26	27
33/6	11	15	18	21	23	25	26	27	28
34/6	11	15	18	21	23	25	27	28	29
36/6	11	15	19	22	24	26	28	29	30
39/6	11	15	19	22	25	27	29	31	32
40/6	11	15	19	22	25	27	29	31	32
42/6	11	15	19	22	25	27	29	31	33
44/6	11	16	20	23	26	28	30	32	34
45/6	11	16	20	23	26	29	31	33	35
46/6	11	16	20	23	26	29	31	33	35
47/6	11	16	20	23	26	29	31	33	35
48/6	11	16	20	24	27	30	32	34	36
49/6	11	15	19	23	26	29	31	33	35
53/6	11	16	20	24	27	30	33	35	37
54/6	11	16	20	24	27	30	33	35	37
40/7	13	18	21	24	26	28	30	32	33

Example of Calculation: 36/6 Format

Line 1:	4-7-9-13-18-20	6 numbers used.
Line 2:	7-8-10-22-26-33	1 repeated number (7), 5 new numbers. 11 numbers used
Line 3:	7-10-16-30-32-36	2 repeated numbers (7,10), 4 new numbers. 15 used.
Line 4:	14-19-22-24-26-27	4 new, 2 repeated (22,26). 19 numbers occur. 17 unused.
Line 5:	11-12-13-18-30-35	3 new, 3 repeated (13,18,30) 22 of 36 numbers are used in 5 tickets. 14 unused.

Numbers left after line 5:

```
                1-2-3-X-5-6-X-X-X-XX-XX-XX    XX=used
    XX-XX-15-XX-17-XX-XX-XX-21-XX-23-XX
    25-XX-XX-28-29-XX-31-XX-XX-34-XX-XX
```

Odds of all 6 winning numbers being within this 5-line example are: (36C6)/(22C6)=1 in 26.1 or 3.8%.

B) Average Repeat Numbers Per Random Selection

(Note: 1 Duplicate Number per 2 Tickets—All Formats.)
Number of Tickets Purchased

Format	2	3	4	5	6	7	8	9	10
35/5	1	2	4	6	9	12	15	19	23
40/5	1	2	4	6	8	11	14	17	20
Total	10	15	20	25	30	35	40	45	50
Total	12	18	24	30	36	42	48	54	60
30/6	1	3	6	10	14	18	23	28	33
33/6	1	3	6	9	13	17	22	27	32
34/6	1	3	6	9	13	17	21	26	31
36/6	1	3	5	8	12	16	20	25	30
39/6	1	3	5	8	11	15	19	23	28
40/6	1	3	5	8	11	15	19	23	28
42/6	1	3	5	9	11	15	19	23	27
44/6	1	2	4	7	10	14	18	22	26
45/6	1	2	4	7	10	13	17	21	25
46/6	1	2	4	7	10	13	17	21	25
47/6	1	2	4	7	10	13	17	21	25
48/6	1	2	4	6	9	12	16	20	24
49/6	1	2	5	7	10	13	17	21	25
53/6	1	2	4	6	9	12	15	19	23
54/6	1	2	4	6	9	12	15	19	<u>23</u>
Total	14	21	28	35	42	49	56	63	70
40/7	1	3	7	11	16	21	26	31	37

EXAMPLE: Buy 10 tickets in 54/6 Format; expect <u>23</u> repeat numbers.

C) Missing Numbers By Random Selection

Number of Tickets Purchased

Format	2	3	4	5	6	7	8	9	10
35/5	26	22	19	16	14	12	10	9	8
40/5	31	27	24	21	18	16	14	12	10
30/6	21	15	12	10	8	6	5	4	3
33/6	22	18	15	12	10	8	7	6	5
34/6	23	19	15	13	11	9	7	6	5
36/6	25	21	17	14	12	10	8	7	6
39/6	28	24	20	17	14	12	10	8	7
40/6	29	25	21	18	15	13	11	9	8
42/6	31	27	23	20	17	15	13	11	9
44/6	33	28	24	21	18	16	14	12	10
45/6	34	29	25	22	19	16	14	12	10
46/6	35	30	26	23	20	17	15	13	11
47/6	36	31	27	24	21	18	16	14	12
48/6	37	32	28	24	21	18	16	14	12
49/6	38	34	30	<u>26</u>	23	20	18	16	14
53/6	42	37	33	29	26	23	20	18	16
54/6	43	38	34	30	27	24	21	19	17
40/7	27	22	19	16	14	12	10	8	7

EXAMPLE: Buy 5 tickets in 49/6 Format; on average, <u>26</u> of 49 don't occur.

Table 4

Odds of All Winning Numbers Occuring Within Multiple-Line Bets

(percent in parenthesis)

Five-ticket bet

Format	Random	Matrix
35/5	1 in 28 (2.6)	1 in 6 (16.0)
40/5	1 in 77 (1.3)	1 in 12.5 (8.0)
30/6	1 in 15 (6.5)	1 in 1 (100.0)
33/6	1 in 29 (3.5)	1 in 1.1 (90)
34/6	1 in 34 (2.9)	1 in 2.3 (44)
36/6	1 in 50 (2.0)	1 in 3 (30)
39/6	1 in 43 (2.3)	1 in 6 (18)
40/6	1 in 53 (1.9)	1 in 6 (15.4)
42/6	1 in 71 (1.4)	1 in 9 (11.3)
44/6	1 in 94 (1.1)	1 in 12 (8.4)
46/6	1 in 100 (1.0)	1 in 16 (6.3)
47/6	1 in 111 (.9)	1 in 18 (5.5)
48/6	1 in 125 (.8)	1 in 21 (4.8)
49/6	1 in 143 (.7)	1 in 24 (4.2)
53/6	1 in 200 (.6)	1 in 44 (2.5)
54/6	1 in 200 (.5)	1 in 44 (2.3)
40/7	1 in 53 (1.9)	1 in 2.8 (36)

Six-ticket bet

Format	Random	Matrix
35/5	1 in 21 (4.8)	1 in 2.3 (43.9)
40/5	1 in 42 (2.4)	1 in 5 (21.7)

30/6	1 in 6 (17.0)	1 in 1 (100)(5 tickets)
33/6	1 in 11 (9.1)	1 in 1.1 (90)(5 tickets)
34/6	1 in 13 (7.5)	1 in 2.3 (94)(5 tickets)
36/6	1 in 19 (5.2)	1 in 1 (100)
39/6	1 in 24 (4.1)	1 in 1.1 (92)
40/6	1 in 29 (3.5)	1 in 1.1 (90)
42/6	1 in 38 (2.6)	1 in 2.7 (37)
44/6	1 in 53 (1.9)	1 in 3.6 (276)
46/6	1 in 53 (1.9)	1 in 4.9 (20.5)
47/6	1 in 63 (1.6)	1 in 5.5 (18.1)
48/6	1 in 71 (1.4)	1 in 6.3 (15.9)
49/6	1 in 77 (1.3)	1 in 7 (13.9)
53/6	1 in 63 (1.6)	1 in 12 (8.5)
54/6	1 in 67 (1.5)	1 in 13 (7.5)
40/7	1 in 29 (3.5)	1 in 2.8 (36.0)(5 tickets)

Seven-ticket bet

Format	Random	Matrix
35/5	1 in 10 (10.4)	1 in 1 (100)
40/5	1 in 20 (5.1)	1 in 2 (49)
30/6	1 in 2.6 (38.8)	1 in 1 (100)(5 tickets)
33/6	1 in 4.8 (20.8)	1 in 1.1 (90)(5 tickets)
34/6	1 in 6 (17.1)	1 in 2.7 (44)(5 tickets)
36/6	1 in 8 (11.8)	1 in 1 (100)(6 tickets)
39/6	1 in 18.5 (5.4)	1 in 1.1 (92)(6 tickets)
40/6	1 in 22 (4.6)	1 in 1.1 (90)(6 tickets)
42/6	1 in 29 (3.2)	1 in 1 (100)
44/6	1 in 40 (2.5)	1 in 1.1 (95.9)
46/6	1 in 25 (4.0)	1 in 1.1 (91.3)
47/6	1 in 29 (3.5)	1 in 2 (48.8)
48/6	1 in 32 (3.1)	1 in 2.3 (42.7)
49/6	1 in 37 (2.7)	1 in 2.7 (37.5)
53/6	1 in 38 (2.6)	1 in 4.3 (22.8)
54/6	1 in 43 (2.3)	1 in 5 (20.3)
40/7	1 in 16 (6.4)	1 in 2.8 (36)(5 tickets)

Eight-ticket bets

Format	Random	Matrix
35/5	1 in 5 (20.3)	1 in 1 (100)(7 tickets)
40/5	1 in 10 (10.0)	1 in 1 (100)
30/6	1 in 2 (49.8)	1 in 1 (100)(5 tickets)
33/6	1 in 4 (26.7)	1 in 1.1 (90)(5 tickets)
34/6	1 in 4.5 (22.0)	1 in 2.7 (44)(5 tickets)
36/6	1 in 6.6 (15.2)	1 in 1 (100)(6 tickets)
39/6	1 in 11 (9.1)	1 in 1.1 (92)(6 tickets)
40/6	1 in 13 (7.7)	1 in 1.1 (90)(6 tickets)
42/6	1 in 18 (5.6)	1 in 1 (100)(7 tickets)
44/6	1 in 24 (4.2)	1 in 1.1 (95.5)(7 tickets)
46/6	1 in 13 (7.9)	1 in 1.1 (91.3)(7 tickets)
47/6	1 in 15 (6.8)	1 in 2 (48.8)(7 tickets)
48/6	1 in 17 (6.0)	1 in 1 (100)
49/6	1 in 19 (5.3)	1 in 1 (98)
53/6	1 in 17 (5.9)	1 in 1.9 (53.5)
54/6	1 in 19 (5.2)	1 in 2.1 (47.5)
40/7	1 in 9 (10.9)	1 in 2.8 (36.0)(5 tickets)

Nine-ticket bet

Format	Random	Matrix
35/5	1 in 4 (24.9)	1 in 1 (100)(7 tickets)
40/5	1 in 8 (12.3)	1 in 1 (100)(8 tickets)
30/6	1 in 1.6 (63.4)	1 in 1 (100)(5 tickets)
33/6	1 in 3 (34.0)	1 in 1.1 (90)(5 tickets)
34/6	1 in 3.5 (28.0)	1 in 2.7 (44)(5 tickets)
36/6	1 in 5 (19.3)	1 in 1 (100)(6 tickets)
39/6	1 in 7 (14.6)	1 in 1.1 (92)(6 tickets)
40/6	1 in 8 (12.4)	1 in 1.1 (90)(6 tickets)
42/6	1 in 11 (9.1)	1 in 1 (100)(7 tickets)
44/6	1 in 15 (6.7)	1 in 1.1 (95.5)(7 tickets)
46/6	1 in 8.5 (11.8)	1 in 1.1 (91.3)(7 tickets)
47/6	1 in 9.7 (10.3)	1 in 2 (48.8)(7 tickets)
48/6	1 in 11 (9.0)	1 in 1.1 (100)(8 tickets)
49/6	1 in 13 (7.9)	1 in 1 (98)(8 tickets)
53/6	1 in 12 (8.5)	1 in 1.9 (53.5)(8 tickets)

54/6	1 in 13 (7.5)	1 in 1 (100)
40/7	1 in 7 (14.1)	1 in 2.8 (36)(5 tickets)

Ten-ticket bet

Format	Random	Matrix
35/5	1 in 3.3 (30.3)	1 in 1 (100)(7 tickets)
40/5	1 in 5.6 (18.0)	1 in 1 (100)(8 tickets)
30/6	1 in 1.2 (85.0)	1 in 1 (100)(5 tickets)
33/6	1 in 1.9 (53.6)	1 in 1.1 (90)(5 tickets)
34/6	1 in 2.3 (44.1)	1 in 2.7 (44)(5 tickets)
36/6	1 in 3.3 (30.5)	1 in 1 (100)(6 tickets)
39/6	1 in 4.4 (22.6)	1 in 1.1 (92)(6 tickets)
40/6	1 in 5 (19.2)	1 in 1.1 (90)(6 tickets)
42/6	1 in 7 (14.0)	1 in 1 (100)(7 tickets)
44/6	1 in 10 (10.4)	1 in 1.1 (95.5)(7 tickets)
46/6	1 in 5.8 (17.3)	1 in 1.1 (91.3)(7 tickets)
47/6	1 in 6.6 (15.1)	1 in 2 (48.8)(7 tickets)
48/6	1 in 7.6 (13.2)	1 in 1 (100)(8 tickets)
49/6	1 in 8.6 (11.6)	1 in 1.1 (98)(8 tickets)
53/6	1 in 8.3 (12.0)	1 in 1.9 (53.5)(8 tickets)
54/6	1 in 9.3 (10.7)	1 in 1 (100)(9 tickets)
40/7	1 in 4.4 (22.9)	1 in 2.8 (36)(5 tickets)

Example: In a 40/6 lottery; only one in every 5 players who buy 10 tickets per random selection will have all 6 winning numbers within 10 lines. Whereas; per matrix methods—1 in every 1.1 will have all 6 winning numbers; but within only 6 lines! Or, expressed in percent: If you buy 10 tickets in a 40/6 lottery by random selection, there is only a 19.2% chance that you will have all 6 winning numbers. Whereas with matrix method–there is a 90% chance you will have all 6 winning numbers; but within only 6 lines! (A better chance of winning! Plus you save money!)

Table

5

The Real Cost of a Chance to Win!

	Average $5 Bet		Best Matrix Bet	
	5-Line Controlled @ 2 numbers Less Than	**5-Line**	**5-Line**	
Format	**Random**	**Random**	**Matrix**	
35/5	262.31	139.59	30.55	7.00 (7-Line)
40/5	531.68	282.94	61.92	8.00 (8-Line)
30/6	159.93	76.60	5.00	5.00 (5-Line)
36/6	358.94	179.47	16.40	6.00 (6-Line)
40/6	495.15	257.22	32.32	11.82 (6-Line)
42/6	*676.70*	*351.53*	*44.17*	*7.00 (7 line)*
44/6	650.44	349.64	59.44	9.42 (7-Line)
46/6	863.08	463.95	78.88	12.50 (7-Line)
47/6	989.38	531.84	90.42	14.33 (7-Line)
48/6	822.34	455.86	103.33	8.00 (8-Line)
49/6	1,288.50	692.63	117.75	9.12 (8-Line)
54/6	1,730.74	959.43	217.48	9.00 (9-Line)
40/7	546.59	269.33	13.86	13.86 (5-Line)
54/6	865.37	479.72	108.74	4.50 (9-Line)

Look at the 42/6 format: the 7-line Matrix has all 42 numbers, so all 6 winning numbers will appear in your Matrix. At $1.00 per line, you have a chance to win for $7.00. With the 5-line Matrix chances are that only 1 in 8.834 Matrices will have all 6 winning numbers. (42C6)/(30C6)=8.834. So your cost here is 8.834 x $5= $44.17 for a chance to win. Looking at the 5-line Random Selection we find that only 1 in 70.306 sets of tickets have all the winning numbers. (42C6)/(22C6)=70.306. $5 x 70.306= $351.53 per chance to win!

In this 5-line Random Selection we would expect to find 22 non-duplicated numbers in the 5 lines. Adding 2 additional duplicate numbers per every 5 lines has this effect: (42C6)/(20C6) which means that only 1 in 135.34 sets will have all the winning numbers. 135.34 x $5= $676.70 per chance to win!

At present, virtually all lottery chances are sold at prices in the left two columns. You can also buy "a chance to win" at prices in the last column!